FACING MILLENNIAL MIDNIGHT

The **Y2K** Crisis
Confronting America
and the World

HAL LINDSEY
& CLIFF FORD

WESTERN FRONT
PUBLISHING

FACING MILLENNIAL MIDNIGHT

ISBN 1-888848-29-4
Published by WESTERN FRONT LTD., Beverly Hills, CA
Interior design by Koechel Peterson & Associates, Minneapolis, Minnesota
Manufactured in the United States of America

Introduction

+ + +

Over the past few months, we have begun to hear the term Y2K used more often in the mainstream media, but most of us don't really have a sense of just what it means to us. By now, virtually everyone knows that the Millennium Bug has something to do with computers and dates, but it seems so *inconsequential*—especially for those people who don't even own a computer, or use one at work.

The street vendor selling hot dogs in a busy downtown district probably thinks that the Y2K computer bug is not his problem. After all, you don't need a computer to make a hot dog. You don't need a computer to maintain an inventory that you can have completely restocked at the local supermarket. "So how can the Millennium Bug possibly impact me?" our hot dog vendor might think.

To answer the question, one merely needs to take a look at the hot dog vendor's clientele. Most of them are employees who work in the office buildings in the downtown area. Bankers, insurance people, government employees, corporate types, but all with one common denominator. All of *their* jobs rely in some way on their office desktops and mainframe computer systems. If those computers don't work, neither will the employees that the hot dog vendor relies on for his living. So, although our hot dog vendor wouldn't know a desktop computer from an Atari game machine, Y2K will have a direct impact on his life.

We have been alarmed at the potential threat posed by public ignorance of the dangers of a Y2K computer meltdown. We have already produced several video documentaries on the subject, and Y2K has been at the center of a number of *International Intelligence Briefing* Special Reports for our television program on the Trinity Broadcasting Network. But we've come to believe that we just aren't doing enough.

It's virtually impossible to convey the complete picture of what the Millennium Bug can do, or how to prepare yourself for it, in a half-hour TV report or even a one-hour special video. Even some of the books already on the market fall short of presenting the full picture.

When we began to plan this book, we tried to think of a way that we could *personalize* the threat, to somehow transport the reader across the Millennium Milestone, away from the comfort of the late 20th century and into a world where the old rules no longer apply.

To do this, we decided to open the first few chapters with a novelette, chronicling the first few days of the new millennium through the eyes of a kind of "Joe Everyman" and his family. We wanted to bring you along for a firsthand peek at just what New Year's Day, 2000, might be like if the Millennium Bug is not squashed in time.

To make it believable, we deliberately elected a "middle of the road" scenario for our fictional family. Our story is based on what we believe is the most likely "best-case scenario" based on the current state of Y2K preparedness. In reality, the world that the Ryan Tyler family awakens to on January 1, 2000, is nowhere near as bad as many experts expect it to be.

As you read the following pages, together with the documented evidence and government readiness charts for the Year 2000, keep in mind that we are presenting the *optimistic* view. It could be much worse than we envision.

HAL LINDSEY
CLIFF FORD

Chapter One

HAPPY
NEW YEAR

January 1, 2000, 7:10 AM

When he woke up, it was dark. Something wasn't quite right, but it took a second to complete the journey—from the upcoming vacation trip to Florida that he had been dreaming of—to that first awareness that it was only a dream. Then reality came into focus, not in the slow, lethargic way it usually does on holiday mornings, but instantaneously, with crystal clarity. It was cold. Really, really cold. Ryan couldn't understand. When he went to bed last night, he made sure all the windows were closed and locked. The light was out on the electric blanket controller. What was wrong with that furnace?

Ryan groaned. He'd skipped the pre-season preventive maintenance service this year. The stock market crash in late October had really put a dent in the family nest egg and they made a list of those expenses they could cut. Preventive maintenance seemed, at the time, to be an expense they could put off. It was a game of financial Russian roulette that had taken place all across America since the Crash.

Stupid, he thought. *To save a lousy sixty-nine bucks then, I've got to freeze until I can round up a service guy who'll come out on New Year's Day.* Ryan grimaced under the inadequate bedclothes.

Sixty-nine bucks started to sound like a bargain. He looked over at Valerie, who was still asleep. She was from Los Angeles and hated the western New York winters. She hated to get out of bed on cold winter mornings, so she always went to bed bundled up like a Russian *babushka*. It was mostly psychosomatic. Bundled up like she was, even the icy cold of the still, dark room didn't wake her. And, by the way, why was it so dark? The bathroom light in the hall was out, and the street light outside the bedroom window wasn't casting its usual ugly yellow glare on the bedroom wall.

As he huddled under the blankets, Ryan noticed something else, but it took him awhile to place what it was. It was too quiet. None of the usual sounds were there. Ryan loved his house; he thought of it almost as a living thing. Often at night he would lie awake and listen to the sounds of his home "breathing." The ever-present, subliminal hum of electric power, not quite identifiable when present, was eerily noticeable when it was gone. It was as if his house had died. Ryan sat bolt upright. *Must be a power failure,* he thought. He got out of bed as quietly as he could, considering the cold. *No point in waking Val right now,* he thought. *She doesn't know she's cold, yet. Time enough to hear her complaining later.*

He hit the floor in a curious half tip-toe, half running gait, arms crossed, hugging himself for warmth as he shrugged into his terrycloth bathrobe and slippers. He pulled the robe around him, wrapped himself in a blanket from the linen closet, and slipped down the stairs. Ryan looked out the window into the front yard. It was a winter wonderland! Freshly fallen snow—several feet of it—blanketed his neighborhood. It was a heavy snowfall, but nothing particularly unusual. Snowfalls this heavy happened several times during the course of a normal winter—more often during a cold winter like this year. Ryan loved winter, and he loved the snow. But right now, as he shivered in the cold of his living room, he longed for June.

Well, he thought, *I'd better get cracking before the house gets any colder.* The power couldn't have been off for more than five or six hours—the house, while cold, was still warmer than it would have been if the power had been off all night. The sun was beginning to come up, revealing a clear, crisp, cloudless winter sky. Despite the cold, the sun's radiant heat, reflected off the fresh snow, would keep it from getting much colder inside until after dark.

Ryan looked longingly at the now useless coffeemaker and wished himself an ironic "Happy New Year."

9:15 AM

They sat huddled on the living room couch: Val in the middle, Ryan and 16-year-old Mikey on either side, shivering under the pile of blankets wrapped around them. They hadn't just awakened to a new year or a new century. It was beginning to look as though they had awakened to a whole new world. Technologically, today bore more resemblance to 1900 than it did to 2000. This was supposed to be Day One of the "new era of mankind" promised by the Secretary General of the UN at the kickoff of the worldwide, UN sponsored "Global 2000 New Millennium Gala." The emergency family planning session had so far yielded one workable suggestion. Mikey's plan to huddle together for warmth wasn't exactly a high-tech solution, but it was the only one that had worked, so far.

Val's first suggestion had been to call Ryan's brother across town. Maybe the power outage was only affecting their part of town. Ryan picked up the phone and dialed the number. The line was busy. He hung up and called the power company. Another busy signal. He tried the gas company. Same thing. Without electricity, they couldn't get any information from TV or radio.

Ryan had already braved the snow to run next door to the Murphy's house. Pat answered the door in the new uniform of the day—a blanket wrapped around him, over his head, with only his face showing. "I don't know, either," Pat said. "We woke up in the dark as well. We haven't been able to get anybody on the phone, either. Justin has a battery-powered TV set that we got him for Christmas. We tried that, and today we can't get anything tuned in. It's a funny thing. It was working fine last night when we went to bed." Pat grinned. "Maybe it's the Millennium Bug we've being hearing about for the past year."

"Yeah, right," Ryan said. "And maybe all those government experts were just lying to us when they said it was much ado about nothing. More likely, the snow just snapped a few power and phone lines. Or somebody slid their car into a utility pole. Listen, Pat, you got any way to heat up some water for coffee?"

"No, but even if I did, there's no water. Wonder what is going on."

The Tylers sat silently on the couch, shivering. Nobody wanted to speak, as if breathing into the cold room would waste the precious warmth they had accumulated by huddling under the heavy pile of blankets over them.

"Well, we can't just sit here," Ryan announced finally. "Everybody get dressed as warmly as you can, and let's drive over to Roy's." Roy Tyler lived on the other side of town, in a new subdivision. During the last weather-related power outage, Roy's subdivision was the only part of town that still had electricity and heat. Unlike the older parts of town, the subdivision was serviced by underground cables for electricity and telephone service.

9:45 AM

While his family stood in the doorway, Ryan struggled with the frozen locks on the car door. It had taken him 10 minutes just to clear the snow off the car with a broom. The fine, granular snow whipped up his sleeves and down his neck as he swept it off the car. Despite the cold, by the time he was done, he was perspiring from the effort. Together with the now-melted snow inside his clothing, Ryan was wet, cold, and cranky by the time he was able to finally get inside the car. The snowplows had still not made an appearance on his street, but he was confident he could navigate the three miles across town once he got onto a main street. He put the key in the ignition and turned it. The engine turned over slowly at first. After a couple of seconds it began to turn over normally, but wouldn't start. He pumped the accelerator and tried again. Nothing. After trying for several more minutes, he gave up. *No point in killing the battery,* he thought. He slammed the door angrily, and stumbled headlong into a snowdrift as he attempted to turn too quickly in the deep snow. By the time he got back into the house, he was wet, cold, and seething with unreasoning anger. Boy, did he need a cup of coffee!

"We've got to find out what's going on. Pat said something about the Millennium Bug. I thought that was all solved."

Ryan looked ridiculous; a little pile of snow formed a peak on the top of his head. Val and Mikey could see Ryan was on the edge—not a good time to laugh. "I never checked. Maybe I can get some news on the car radio." As he turned, Mikey said, "I've got that shortwave transistor radio you bought me last Christmas. It runs on batteries." He looked sheepish. "The batteries are low, though. I usually run it off the adapter."

Ryan looked outside. "Go get it."

Mikey got the radio, but the batteries were completely dead. After some searching, Val and Ryan found the right size batteries in the TV remote control. After a few seconds of trying to figure out the tuner, Ryan handed it to Mikey and said, "Find something."

Glad to feel useful, Mikey took the radio and soon picked up a scratchy Emergency Broadcast Signal from the government.

"The biggest headache right now is the loss of the power grid along the eastern seaboard. FEMA is coordinating a massive effort by software engineers to isolate and repair the faulty codes. The failure was believed to be caused by the failure of forgotten embedded processors in the relay system that incorrectly interpreted the date changeover from nine-nine to double-zero. The built in failsafe systems, designed to prevent nuclear power accidents, sent a message to the main computer that ordered the power grid shut down.[1] Engineers are working on the problem, and partial power will be restored to some areas within several days. Other parts of the country may remain without power for longer periods of time. The President has, by Executive Order, declared a national state of emergency. The director of FEMA, under the terms of Executive Order 12919,[2] has declared the United States under martial law. Civil liberties are

---

1 To a degree that surprises non-specialists, embedded systems routinely have recourse to time stamps. The chip may contain a rule like this: If generator 23 hasn't been serviced for six months, shut it down and import electricity from the neighboring state.

2 This order, signed by the President in 1994, takes the authority of 11 preceding Executive Orders and consolidates them into one document that essentially places the government outside the system of Constitutional checks and balances for the duration of a declared emergency. By its invocation, martial law is an effective reality and the supreme law of the land.

temporarily suspended, and a national curfew has been imposed. All persons are ordered to stay in their homes until further notice. Armed federal troops will be patrolling urban areas to prevent looting. This is not a drill. Stay tuned to this frequency for further updates from the Emergency Broadcast System." The voice was replaced by the familiar Emergency Broadcast tone.

COUNTING DOWN TO MILLENNIAL MIDNIGHT
+ + +

Throughout this book, we will follow the Tyler family as it attempts to cope with the Y2K Bug. The plan is to show just exactly how the failure of the world's computer network will affect the average family, even if they don't even own a computer. In essence, this is two books in one— a novel about the coming computer crisis and information from experts in the field that will explain exactly what the Y2K bug is, what it will do, and why it can't be completely repaired in time to prevent at least some of the disruptions that our fictional family will have to cope with. The experts are divided on just how severe the crisis will be, but nobody is denying the fact that there will indeed be a crisis. In our story, we are presenting the worst-case scenario. Y2K may not impact quite as severely as we anticipate, but, if you are prepared for the worst, then anything less than that will be a pleasant surprise.

More than two thirds of worldwide companies in food processing, farming, government services, education, and other high-risk industries are expected to experience at least one mission-critical system failure due to year 2000 computer problems, according to new research conducted by Gartner Group Inc., of Stamford, Conn. In addition, from 30 percent to 50 percent of companies in all industries worldwide will experience similar Y2K-related computer failures, Gartner officials say. Lou Marcoccio, Gartner's Y2K research director, says that the semiconductor industry is also ill-prepared for the new millennium, along with many of the world's governments. Gartner research shows that nearly 23 percent of companies worldwide have not started to evaluate the impact the Y2K bug could have on their businesses, even though it can require up to 30 months to fully repair a major systems glitch. Many companies are already seeing Y2K failures, primarily in their projection and forecasting systems. The study also shows that even among companies that are implementing Y2K fixes, only half will test the systems before putting them into production. This will offer companies little assurance that the fixes will fully address Y2K problems when they occur. Gartner based its findings on a quarterly survey of 15,000 companies and government agencies in 87 countries.[3]

On the other hand, failing to prepare for the worst-case scenario could mean the difference between life or death. As we progress, you will see that this is not an exaggeration.

What Is Y2K?
+ + +

Y2K is simply an abbreviation for Year 2000. During the 1960s and 1970s, when computing was still in its embryonic stages, computer programming was a very expensive and time-consuming process.

The Year 2000 problem is essentially the result of a shortcut and money-saving trick that turned into a shortsighted and very expensive logistical nightmare. Here is how it happened. When the majority of today's computer systems were first created,

3 "Gartner Sees Problems Coming," *PC Week*, September 21, 1998.

the original designers were forced to decide how to define dates in computer data. Stored in databases and files, this data was dependent on a date value in order to function. This date value was to be defined by assigning a number to the day, month, and year that it represented. Sounds simple enough. Unfortunately, when the time came to assign numbers to these dates, the programmers decided to define the year field using a two-digit rather than a four-digit representation. Here's an example of what the programmers did. Using the "day/month/year" format and a two-digit year representation, the date February 15, 1960, was assigned the numbers 15/02/60 (with the "19" before the "60" being assumed). Obviously, this assumption would only remain true until December 31, 1999; after that date—from January 1, 2000, until the next century—the two digits before the year representation will no longer be "19" but "20." Consequently, from this standpoint, any date into and beyond the Year 2000 will have a different logic to it than any date in the 1900s, and any computer that uses this logic will be unable to compare the two. This will result in any of a number of errors, ranging from miscalculations to computer stoppages and malfunctions.[4]

Today, one can sit down at a personal computer, look at the monitor, and directly input information into the computer hard disk drive from the computer keyboard. But in 1969, the process was much more complicated. Programmers would write the code in one of almost 500 different proprietary computer languages, like COBOL or FORTRAN. The code would then be sent to a keypunch operator. The keypunch operator would input the information, which would be punched into a card. Remember when computer generated checks carried the warning "Do not bend, fold or mutilate" printed on the check itself? The reason for the warning was because the holes in the check allowed a computer to read the information printed on it. Each keypunch card contained 88 characters, or "bytes" of information. In other words, the information that a single, modern 1.44 megabyte floppy disk could carry would require a keypunch operator to input 88 times 1,440,000 keystrokes! The final product would be 87,500 individual keypunch cards. That was just the beginning of the process. From there, the cards

---

4 "What Is Y2K?" Adam Kaplan, *The Westergaard 2000 Group.*

would be fed through an EAM, or Electronic Accounting Machine that would collate, or sort, the cards into a predetermined order encoded on the keypunch cards by the programmer. Once the 87,500 cards were all sorted and boxed, the information would be transferred to a spool of magnetic tape about the size of a dinner plate. A job this size would require a half dozen or more of these tapes. Each one would be loaded onto a tape drive about the size of a refrigerator. The operator would run the program, and the completed data would be printed out on bifold paper using a dot matrix printer about half the size of an apartment dumpster. Remember, it took all that equipment to run a program that today would fit on a 3.5 inch floppy disk. For this reason, any shortcuts that would reduce the number of keystrokes necessary and reduce the amount of memory necessary to run the program would save thousands of hours and multiple thousands of dollars.[5]

_____

5 Using the model to calculate the cumulative savings through 1995 from an application created in 1963, we concluded that such a system "has saved between $650,000 and $1.5 million per gigabyte of total storage (in 1995 dollars), depending on how quickly storage equipment was upgraded. For the 25 years from 1972 to 1997, the comparable figures are $35,000 to $75,000 per gigabyte, and for the 15 years from 1983 to 1997, $600 to $1,250 (*Year 2000 Problem: Strategies and Solutions from the Fortune 100*, International Thomson Press, p. 54; www.year2000.unt. edu/book).

One of those shortcuts involved only encoded data that was absolutely necessary. Since virtually all computer programs operate according to an internal clock, codes representing dates were the most replicated throughout the process. Programmers adopted the convention of using a date format that dropped the first two digits from the year portion of the date. For example, February 3, 1969, would be input as 03/02/69. Removing these two keystrokes in the date eliminated literally millions of keystrokes for the keypunch operator, reduced the number of keypunch cards that had to be handled at the various stages of the programming and computer operations process, resulting in savings of millions of dollars per year. This is the DD-MM-YY format that is in use today in most of the world's computers. At the time, nobody foresaw the consequences down the road. Few programmers believed the programs they were writing in 1969 would still be in use today. Neil Armstrong had planted the American flag on the face of the moon. The technical revolution was just getting started, and it wasn't too far-fetched back then to anticipate that by the year 2000, we would drive to work in flying cars, take our vacations in outer space, cure the common cold, and eliminate poverty. Early programmers never dreamed that subsequent generations would simply overlay new programming over the template they were at that time developing.

The glitch was passed on from one generation of programmers to the next. So today, businesses and governments around the world are scrambling to fix a problem that threatens everything from the national electrical power grid to some VCRs. Even Alan Greenspan, perhaps the most influential voice in the world economy, added to the problem. In the 1960s, he was designing computer programs for the New York City-based economic consulting firm he headed. "I'm one of the culprits who created this problem," Greenspan said in July during testimony before the Senate banking committee. "I used to write those programs back in the '60s and '70s and was so proud of the fact that I was able to squeeze a few elements of space out of my program by not having to put 19 before the year."[6]

---

6 "Chances to Fix Year 2000 Problem Squandered for Decades," *Fort Worth Star Telegram,* by David Hayes and Finn Bullers.

The Hundred-Year Gap
+ + +

What is being called "The Millennium Bug" is simply what will happen when the calendar turns over from 1999 to 2000. For example, December 31, 1999, would read 31/12/99. Therefore January 1, 2000, would be read by computers the world over as 01/01/00. And that's the problem! To a computer, that means January 1, 1900. Now, why should that be important? Let's consider a few things. Railroads, for example. In the United States, the rail system is 100 percent computer dependent. Track schedules are maintained by computer—meaning, the computer ensures that two trains don't come roaring down the same track from opposite directions. When the date rolls, the mainframe computers operating the nation's rail systems will think it is January 1, 1900. Therefore, a northbound train at 11:59 PM December 31, 1999, would disappear at the stroke of midnight! At least, as far as the computer is concerned. At 12:01 January 1, 2000, the mainframe would not expect that train to be there for another 100 years. What conductor would move his train under those circumstances?

Air traffic control computers could not accept flight plans for flights that originate on December 31, 1999, and are scheduled to land after midnight

2000. From the computer's point of view, that landing would have taken place 100 years before departure! Trains move food and necessities. Airliners move people. Without functioning computer systems, nothing moves anywhere. The aircraft themselves will be affected. Large airliners often have 500 or more different on-board computer systems governing everything from take-offs and landings to navigational systems. All are date sensitive. In November 1997, KLM (Royal Dutch Airlines) became the first of what undoubtedly will be many airlines to announce they will ground their aircraft at midnight, December 31, 1999.

> "A set of crucial computers in the nation's air traffic control system should not be used beyond December 1999 because they may not operate reliably when the date rolls over to January 1, 2000, and there is no way to predict the effect on air traffic, according to IBM, which built the computers."[7]

It's hard to imagine a more date dependent system than Social Security. Dates of birth, dates of employment, dates of eligibility, etc., all become future at the stroke of 12:00, because the

---

7 *New York Times*, January 13, 1998.

computer will believe it's 1900. All recipients will
not yet have been born, contributed premiums,
or be part of the system when the internal calendar clicks over to 01/01/00. The problem is enormous, and there isn't nearly enough time to
reprogram all the systems.

"The General Accounting Office [warned]
that the Social Security Administration
(SSA) faces a possible computer crash in
the year 2000 because the agency has not
started analyzing or fixing several crucial
systems affected by the Year 2000 software
glitch. Among the systems not yet ana-
lyzed are most of the 54 computer systems
that operate state disability determination
services, according to the GAO, the watch-
dog arm of Congress. The GAO also said
the Social Security Administration has not
developed adequate contingency plans in
case its computers are not fixed in time.
*The SSA has long been touted as the federal
agency that is most keenly aware of the year
2000 problem* [emphasis mine]. The
agency, whose mission critical systems col-
lectively had been thought to have about
34 million lines of computer code, began
making year 2000 repairs almost a decade
ago. 'If Social Security, which we've thought

had everything under control, really doesn't, that raised new questions about other agencies,' said a Congressional staffer. According to the GAO, private contractors hired by the SSA to fix the year 2000 glitch on 42 of 54 state disability determination services computers discovered 33 million additional lines of code that need to be tested, and where necessary, fixed. Analyzing and fixing the problem likely will be a massive undertaking. In just one office, the GAO said it found 600,000 lines of code in 400 programs that operate the disability system."[8]

Everyone is hoping some whiz kid will invent a "magic bullet" that will deal with the Millennium Bug in time. That makes as much sense as planning your budget based on lottery winnings—before the draw takes place. To fix the Y2K problem, mainly written in a now-obsolete language called COBOL, programmers need to search billions of lines of code, a line at a time, correcting each to recognize the new dates. It is estimated it would take 11,000 COBOL programmers three years to fix just the Social Security mainframe problems. At the time of this writing,

---

8 *The Washington Post,* November 5, 1997.

there aren't that many available COBOL programmers in the whole world. All in all, it would
take 300,000 COBOL programmers to fix just the
US government's mainframes by the year 2000.
And not all the mainframes are programmed in
COBOL. Some are programmed in even lesser-
known archaic computer languages. The US Office
of Management and Budget reported in 1997 that
even the Federal Emergency Management Agency
(FEMA)—whose mission is to take over in a crisis,
won't be on-line after midnight, January 1, 2000!

> "FEMA (Federal Emergency Management
> Agency) will take the lead in assuring that
> the federal government is doing all that is
> necessary to be ready should serious dis-
> ruptions occur," says John Koskinen,
> chairman of the president's Y2K Council.
> And what does Fox Mulder's favorite gov-
> ernment agency plan to do when your elec-
> tricity and telephones don't work? "FEMA
> has performed no assessments of the Y2K
> computer problem on the telecommunica-
> tions and electric power infrastructures,"
> says James Lee Witt, director of the agency.
> "FEMA has no contingency plans specifi-
> cally designed to address network interop-
> erability or embedded chip failures in either
> the telecommunications or electric power

industries." Instead, it seems, FEMA's role will be to coordinate a population pacification program—better known as martial law.[9]

Greatest Crisis in History?

+ + +

A new joke making the rounds on the Internet would be much funnier if only it was less accurate. "If builders built houses the way programmers wrote programs, the first woodpecker would have destroyed civilization." It wouldn't be stretching the point to argue the Y2K problem could well become the greatest worldwide crisis in history. Without computers, the global economy would melt down faster than butter in a frying pan. Okay, you made your mortgage payment on December 15, 1999. Next one is due, oh, in about 100 years or so. Great for you, but what about the bank holding the note? Could you even *sell* your house after January 1, 2000? When is your car payment due again? Whose car does it become after midnight, January 1, 2000? And when did you say your savings bonds mature? Or your stocks, or whatever? If all the records say it's now 100 years ago, you are basically wiped out in every area

9 "Between the Lines," September 17, 1998, by Joseph Farah.

where dates are an important element. Which is to say, everything you don't already own, you probably never will. All you've saved is locked away in a vault that won't open for 100 years.

> "Banks and other financial institutions generally will go bonkers if they don't fix the [Y2K] problem. In the worst case scenario, the entire financial infrastructure, including the stock market, will go haywire. Balances, records and transactions will be lost. Y2K could be the event that could all but paralyze the planet."[10]

Waking Up in the Dark
+ + +

When the Tyler family woke up on New Year's morning, 2000, the house was dark and cold. The electrical power grid had failed, together with the pumping systems and other computerized delivery systems that supply most homes with natural gas. Just how likely a scenario is that?

> "If the power grid goes down, then it is all over. It doesn't matter if every computer in the country is Y2K compliant if you can't plug it into something. So we are focusing

---

10 *Newsweek,* June 2, 1997, "The Day the World Shuts Down."

first and foremost on utilities and not just power. The water treatment system in every municipality in this country is computer driven and has the potential of being upset because of embedded chips and bad software. Utilities, therefore, are at the top of the list of the things we are addressing in our committee."[11]

Senator Bennett of Utah is the chairman of the Special Senate Committee on the Year 2000 Technological Problem. As chairman of this subcommittee, Bennett is responsible for keeping lawmakers abreast of the progress—or lack of progress—of Y2K compliance efforts in advance of Millennial Midnight. In that capacity, Bennett conducted a survey of the 10 largest electric, gas, and oil utilities in the nation recently to determine their status as to Y2K compliancy. He reported to the Senate that not a single utility company was certain that suppliers, vendors, and servicers who make up the gas and electricity delivery systems would be Y2K compliant. Even worse, none of them had even developed a Y2K contingency plan just in case the current system failed. Only

---

11 Sen. Robert Bennett, chairman of the Special Senate Committee on the Year 2000 Technology Problem, June 12, 1998.

two had even assessed their automated systems, and one utility didn't even know how many lines of code it needed to check, let alone having already begun to repair the faulty lines. And even if all America's utility companies were Y2K compliant—which they are not—there is still no guarantee that America can count on its utility supply after Millennial Midnight. Many of our utility suppliers depend on foreign oil to maintain operations. If those foreign suppliers aren't ready for Y2K, the production and delivery of that oil might be interrupted at the source. It won't make much difference if Con-Edison is Y2K compliant, if an interrupted oil supply makes it impossible to generate electricity. Another Senator, Christopher Dodd of Connecticut, painted an even gloomier picture when he testified at the same hearing.

> "When I was back in Connecticut last weekend, I noticed a fair amount of advertising for New Year's Eve 1999 in which the question was asked: 'Where do you want to go for New Year's? Make your plans today!' While I don't know where anyone else wants to be, let me suggest three places you don't want to be: in an elevator, in an airplane or in a hospital. . . . The fact is that with less than 18 months to go, I am very

concerned that we are going to face serious economic dislocations from this problem."

The nation's utility companies have all but given up on the concept of Y2K compliance and are instead working toward something that they call "Y2K" readiness. A recent North American Reliability Council (NERC) Y2K report explains the difference:

> "Y2K Ready means a system or component has been determined to be suitable for continued use into the Year 2000. Note that this is not necessarily the same as Y2K Compliant, which implies fully correct date manipulations. Consistent with practices across other industries, the NERC assessment process has adopted the term Y2K Ready and does not use the term Y2K Compliant."[12]

One expert who examined the NERC report is Roleigh Martin. On October 1, 1998, Martin gave his assessment of what the NERC report will mean to Ryan Tyler and his family on January 1, 2000, and of the vast gulf that exists between the terms, "compliance" and "readiness."

---

12 North American Reliability Council Report, page 25, August 17, 1998.

This means that their goal is to use a combination of occasional manual workarounds, acceptance of occasional erroneous data outputs, contingency plans, etc., and minimal, mission-critical Y2K mitigation to ensure that they are able to produce power in 2000 and beyond. They are not projecting the same smooth operational stance they are operating under presently. Because the industry typically works with electronic controls that often have shelf lives of approximately 15 years, their suppliers and the utilities should have been demanding Y2K compliance in their upgraded equipment in the mid-1980s. With software, one can wait until the early part of the 1990-2000 decade to responsibly start a software Y2K project. However, one cannot responsibly wait this long with hardware that typically has a 15-year lifespan and needs upgrading. But with the utilities, they generally waited until 1997-1998 to start their embedded systems Y2K project—what negligence and oversight![13]

-----

13 "Will We Have Electricity in the Year 2000?" Roleigh Martin—Y2K *Today* http://www.y2ktoday.com

When our friend Ryan Tyler tried to use the telephone, all he could get was a busy signal. Even if the telephone service is not interrupted by Y2K-related failures (which is a best-case scenario, and also extremely unlikely), millions of homes across America will wake up freezing in the dark. Those millions will undoubtedly run immediately to the telephone to call their local utility to find out what is going on. The busy signal Tyler kept getting is not without precedent. Each year on Mother's Day, millions of sons and daughters pick up the phone to call Mom. During peak times, callers would hear the computerized message, "Due to the high volume of traffic, all circuits are temporarily busy. Please try your call again later." The telephone overload on New Year's Day, 2000, will make Mother's Day traffic look insignificant by comparison.

Tyler was unable to start his car. Most late model vehicles are equipped with embedded computer chips (more on this later) that regulate the car's ignition system based on the last date of service. Noncompliant chips will misinterpret the date to mean that the automobile hasn't been serviced in at least 100 years and will refuse to allow the vehicle to start as part of their internal fail-safe routine.

Computers are vulnerable to Y2K at three levels. Those levels are **software** and **hardware** (the computer itself and its programs), **embedded chips**, and **embedded systems**.

Embedded chips are microprocessors (small computers) that are found in single, isolated devices like cellular phones, microwave ovens, and pacemakers, and automated systems such as elevators and security systems. Their responsibility is to regulate the basic functioning of these machines—from making sure that pacemakers keep on ticking, to controlling when security alarms go off.

Embedded systems refer to either single or multipurpose computerized devices that are literally embedded within some larger piece of engineering equipment or industrial product. The Year 2000 embedded systems problem deals with embedded systems that are subject to failure because their software is not Year 2000 compliant.

No one knows how many systems will fail or whether single failures could cause a chain reaction, bringing down whole manufacturing lines or even an electrical power grid. But many experts say that some things are almost certain to go haywire.

"I think it is axiomatic that there are going to be power failures due to Y2K," said John Pike, an analyst with the

Federation of American Scientists, a Washington, DC think tank. "The only thing that is uncertain about it is how many are you going to have and the extent to which the problem cascades." The problem with embedded systems is just that—they are embedded. While programmers have relatively easy access to software code and databases, most embedded systems contain "firmware"—code that is hard-wired into the system. Even if technicians can determine that an embedded system's code contains the bug, it most often cannot be rewritten. The system, often consisting of a single postage stamp-sized microprocessor, must be replaced with one that is bug-free. And that is not easy. Older chip designs are hard to come by; the program compiler used to generate the executable code is often out of date and those who knew the compiler have gone on to more lucrative pursuits. Besides, some circuit boards are not designed to have easily removable chips. Often, replacing entire interrelated systems is the only solution. Embedded systems control timing of elevators, pressure in pipelines, and even the functioning of automatic transmissions. Experts say billions were manufactured last year.[14]

Ryan Tyler had hoped to get his family to his brother's home in a newer subdivision, mistakenly believing that the power interruption was localized to his neighborhood. As we have already seen, if the power grid does fail, underground delivery cables will not make any difference. Ryan Tyler and his family ended up doing what most unprepared American families will find themselves doing on January 1, 2000—huddling for warmth under a blanket and trying to figure out their next move. January 1, 2000, falls on a Saturday. For the Tylers—and for you, if you haven't developed a Y2K contingency plan, it will be a very long weekend.

---

14 *Business Today*, November 13, 1998.

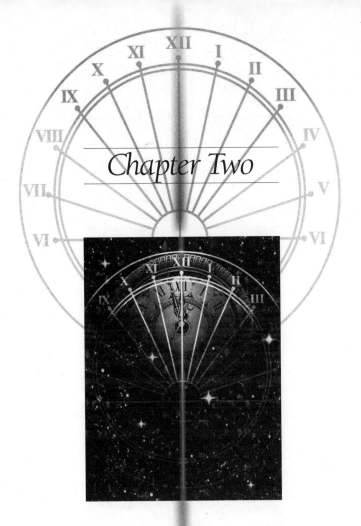

Chapter Two

B y now, the Tylers realized the enormity of the problem facing them. To all intents and purposes, they found themselves trapped in a technological time warp. All around them were the reminders of life in the 21st century: appliances, automobiles, indoor plumbing, electric lighting, a big screen television set, four telephones . . . all completely useless. Nothing worked. Saturday's busy signal had, by Sunday morning, been replaced by dead silence. The overloaded circuits eventually just shut themselves down, or burned out, or whatever. Who knew? And, at this point, who cared why? It was enough to know the phones had joined the rest of the utilities in electronic limbo.

After huddling for most of Saturday, the Tylers decided to revert to the transportation mode best suited to the "brave, new world of the 21st century." They bundled up and walked the three miles across town to Ryan's brother's home, arriving midafternoon. It was a miserable walk—none of the roads or sidewalks had been plowed, and walking three miles in two feet of unplowed snow was more work than walking three times that distance on dry ground. And it was cold. Ryan couldn't remember ever being this cold.

Partly because there was nowhere to get warm. The closest thing to warmth was being out of the wind inside the house, huddled under a blanket with Val and Mikey. But Ryan knew it would be much worse once the sun went down. Hoping that maybe the power was still on across town, they decided to make the trip.

They were wrong. The utilities were out all over town, including the new subdivision. But, at least, Roy had heat. Although the house was new, Ryan's brother had installed a wood burning stove in November. Ryan remembered laughing at Roy at the time.

"Broski, this is a brand-new house. It's a model for the new millennium. You plug a tube into the wall, and it's a vacuum cleaner. You've got central heat and air, you don't have to worry about some idiot slamming into a utility pole, or an ice storm, or even a hurricane knocking out your power. It's all protected underground. Why in the world would you put in a wood-burning stove? It's going to cost you a fortune for fire-wood, and you'll end up with wood splinters, bugs, and who knows what else inside your house. Live a little, Broski. You have arrived. You're living the American dream. Relax."

Secretly, Ryan thought Roy was just a little nuts; he was one of those guys who just couldn't stop planning for the worst, even in the best of times. Sure, the market had crashed in October, but Roy was a computer technician. It didn't matter how bad the economy got, he'd always have a job. The same day Ryan got his layoff notice, Roy got a big bonus. Ryan was always a little jealous of his younger brother, so he was particularly critical sometimes. Especially when Roy put on his "know-it-all" attitude.

"Rye," Roy said then, "if what I've been hearing about the Year 2000 bug is true, it'll be worth the time, effort, and money I've put in to installing this thing. And if I'm wrong, well, I like the smell of firewood. Having a backup ready never killed anybody. Not having a plan has killed lots of people. You know what I always say—if you snooze, you lose."

Oh, please, Ryan thought, *not another homily. Does he have a book by his bed called* Shallow Homilies for Every Occasion *or what?*

Ryan felt like the grasshopper from the old Aesop fable. In the fable, as the ant toiled to prepare for winter, the grasshopper squandered his opportunity to make hay while the sun shined. When winter came, the grasshopper was unprepared and ended up begging from the ant.

Because Roy was a computer technician, he had recognized early on the potential for chaos in the event of a global computer meltdown. He had laid in a supply of water, dehydrated food, a wood burning stove, firewood, first aid supplies and even a gasoline generator. He had a 50 gallon gasoline tank installed behind his garage and a rationing plan and backup batteries that would provide him with electricity for two hours a day for three months. He'd tried to convince Ryan of the potential, but his brother preferred to believe the CNN version in which any disruption would be sporadic, inconsequential and short-lived. Although it had only been three days, it seemed an eternity. Information was still sketchy about the scope of the disruption, so nobody knew yet just how sporadic the energy crisis was or how many communities were affected. But it was far from inconsequential as far as the Tyler family was concerned. It was only Monday, but the grocery store shelves had been stripped clean by those lucky enough to have some cash on hand. On Sunday morning, Roy and Ryan made their way to the local supermarket to pick up some perishables, like bread and milk, before they were all gone. Bread was going for $60.00 a loaf, milk $45.00 a quart. Hand-lettered signs offered an alternative price of $1.75 and $1.50—provided they were paid for with pre-1964 silver coins. Ryan had seen something like this during the

early days of the 1970s oil embargo. Service stations had this dual pricing scheme—gas at $1.45
or $0.40 a gallon in pre-'64 silver coins.

Banks remained closed, ATM machines were
still dark, but there was nothing left to buy, any-
way. Not with paper money. Roy, who lived each
day like tomorrow was an incipient disaster, had
invested in junk silver coins for years. Ryan
scoffed at him and put his money into the stock
market. Ryan was virtually wiped out in the
October Crash. Roy had accumulated bags of old
silver coins. Nothing special, not collector coins—
just old silver money. They got the last eight loaves
of bread and a gallon and a half of milk.

The nation's computerized transportation network was down. Trains weren't running. Gasoline
was being rationed by those few service stations
who were fortunate enough to have independent
electrical generators. Without a functioning
transportation network, there was no way to
replenish the supply when the available fuel was
all gone. The nation's trucking fleet was idled by
the lack of available fuel. Most gas stations were
completely closed, lacking electricity to pump the
gasoline from their underground tanks to the
pumps. Ryan recognized how fortunate he was to
live in a small town with a large family. If they
lived in one of the anonymous big cities, they

would still be sitting in a cold, dark home until the food ran out. Then what? He shuddered to think of it.

They spent the day settling in; it looked like it would be some time before they went home for any length of time. They were no longer without transportation—Roy had an old snowmobile that he loved to tinker with. It was entirely mechanical; no computer chips, fuel injection, or any other high-tech electronics. Just an old style, mechanical internal combustion system. His old pickup truck was similarly unaffected, although his later model family car was as useless as Ryan's was. They had just returned after going back to pick up some clothes and other personal items to see them through for a few days. Although the snowplows were still not running, the snow had melted somewhat under the bright January sun, and it was possible to follow in the trail blazed by earlier, braver travelers. Many of those earlier pioneers now angled nose first into the drainage ditches lining the roadway, serving as landmarks to guide those who followed later.

Both families were cramped into the two rooms heated by the wood stove. Ryan, Val and Mikey had pallets in one corner of the kitchen, affording a tiny measure of privacy. Roy, Lorna, and his four children had spread out sleeping bags in the living room. The area in the living room around the sofa served as a undeclared common area. They shared the bathroom, which was closed off and unheated. But, thanks to Roy's foresight, they were warm, they had enough food, and, soon, they would turn on the generator for two hours of electricity.

6:00 PM

Roy started the generator, and, in a few minutes, it almost seemed like things were back to normal, apart from the orange extension cords running from the generator in the basement up to the living area where Roy plugged in the TV. The only working television station was a low power, local UHF station that broadcast a weak signal over a jury-rigged transmission antenna.

The news was not good, what there was of it. The Y2K bug struck with a vengeance. At the stroke of midnight, a few systems crashed outright. The IRS computer network was among the first to go dark. But most seemed to continue to function normally. After several hours, and, in a few cases, several days—the apparently unaffected computer networks began to issue conflicting or illogical commands, and things began to cascade out of control. Those computer networks that were Y2K compliant were connected to other, noncompliant systems that they relied on for data. The corrupted commands issued by the noncompliant client systems "infected" the updated systems as effectively as a computer virus. Embedded processor chips in pumping stations, electrical power transmission systems, natural gas pipelines and telephone transmission stations also misinterpreted the maintenance dates and ordered emergency fail-safe shutdown routines that effectively turned off the national power grid. The anchor admitted that the information available was hours old, and there was very little information about how long—or whether—regular energy services might be restored.

Throughout the broadcast, the news announcer stressed that much of the information was unconfirmed, gleaned mostly from ham radio operators across the country and around the world. Big cities like Los Angeles and New York were going up in flames. Rioting and looting were not confined just to the inner city, but to outlying suburbs as well. Police communications networks had completely broken down. Police looked on helplessly as the mayhem continued. Many simply went home to protect their own families. Hundreds of people had reportedly been killed in random acts of violence since the blackout began, although no verifiable numbers were available.

Martial law had been declared, and the National Guard had been given orders to shoot looters on sight. Still the chaos continued. The communications satellites were still inoperable and television, telephone, and cellular telephone services were down. There were unconfirmed reports of nuclear accidents at several US nuclear power plants, but there was no assessment of any damage to the environment.

Not so in Russia, according to the report. All of Russia's aging stable of nuclear generating plants went haywire at the stroke of midnight Saturday. The computer network began issuing contradictory instructions based on its interpretation of maintenance data. The mainframe suddenly became "aware" of the fact that scheduled maintenance was 100 years overdue. The safety protocol routine shut down all operations, some in the middle of delicate subroutines. The abrupt shutdown caused several to meltdown completely, some reportedly as severe as the Chernobyl nuclear disaster in the Ukraine in 1987.

The announcer cautioned his viewers again that the information came from unconfirmed ham radio accounts emanating from inside the Russian Federation. In the Middle East, a ham radio operator who claimed to be in Baghdad said that when the Iraqi government's computer systems began to malfunction, Saddam Hussein interpreted it as a cyberspace attack against him by the Israelis. He ordered the immediate manual launch of his Scud missile arsenal against Israel. Most of the missiles detonated on launch. Several carried nerve gas warheads. Thousands of Iraqi civilians were reported to have died, but again, no reliable casualty statistics were available. Ham radio "reporters" in Israel said none of the missiles struck the Jewish state that they were aware of. A ham radio report from Cyprus said two of what were believed to be missiles reportedly landed in the Mediterranean Sea off the coast of the island.

There was much more news, the announcer said, but the station was also running on generator power, and the enormous draw of the transmission equipment meant they could only generate enough power to operate for 30 minutes at a time. He said the next broadcast would be in 12 hours. The screen then disintegrated into snow as the signal shut down. Roy turned off the TV and sat down without a word, staring unfocused at the opposite wall. Roy's three girls, normally in a state of undeclared war with each other, sat together silently, arms linked. Kenny sat beside his mother as she stroked his hair absently. It was a strange, surrealistic atmosphere in which nothing was familiar; there was no common experience that they could draw on to fully absorb what was happening.

Val and Mikey were in their corner of the kitchen, listening rather than watching. After Roy turned off the television set, Ryan rose and joined his family in the kitchen while he absorbed what he had heard.

Ryan realized that if even a third of what he had heard was actually true, and not just hysterical rumor, the situation was much worse than he could have ever imagined. Not even in his wildest nightmare. But here it was. Thrown back—overnight—into the technological Dark Ages. Where was the government in all this? The only government *he* had seen so far in this crisis was two National Guardsman patrolling the neighborhood earlier in a Jeep. They were both heavily armed and *definitely* gave the impression they were in no mood to be helpful. Their job was to carry out the orders of the Federal Emergency Management Authority, and they wore the black FEMA[15] armbands around the right sleeve of their field jackets so there would be no mistake. FEMA ordered them to maintain order and gave them the authority to use whatever force

---

15 Under the authority of Presidential Executive Order 12919 signed by President Clinton (see end notes).

was necessary—including deadly force—to maintain order, not hand out food stamps or to give friendly, "how to cope with total chaos" advice.

He suddenly felt as helpless as a child. He had always been a self-reliant type, but he was most valuable for what he *knew*, not what he was actually able to accomplish in a physical sense on his own. He made a living knowing *how* to operate the technical marvels of his generation, not how to do the tasks they took over.

Ryan knew how to use technology to *obtain* the necessities of life, not how to grow a tomato or butcher a cow, or even where to get one if he did. He didn't hunt, knew nothing about fishing, and the only tools he could use beyond a hammer and nails required an electrical outlet. He had no money to speak of, and no way to get what little he did have out the bank. His available cash wouldn't cover a loaf of bread at the supermarket—if there was one left.

The Cascade Effect
+ + +

Although the experts are divided somewhat on the scope and intensity of the crisis that will follow Millennial Midnight, they pretty much agree that the most serious damage to the global information systems will not be apparent for several days. That is due to what is called the *cascade effect*. It is this effect that will shut down the global power grid, banking system and other interconnected systems, if *all* aren't ready when the Bug bytes (pun intended).

The electric systems of North America are connected within four large Interconnections. The largest, the Eastern Interconnection, covers the eastern two thirds of North America, including the United States and Canada. The second largest, the Western Interconnection, covers the western one third of the US and Canada, as well as a portion of the Baja California Norte region of Mexico. The other two Interconnections include 1) most of the state of Texas, also known as the ERCOT Region, and 2) the Quebec Interconnection, which covers the province of Quebec, Canada. Each of these four Interconnections is a highly connected network. A major disturbance within one part of an Interconnection will rapidly have an impact throughout the Interconnection and has the potential to cascade the effect to the entire Interconnection. The four Interconnections are for the most part independent from each other, because they are connected by comparatively small high-voltage direct current (HVDC) electrical ties and do not interconnect synchronously. The one notable exception is the major HVDC tie lines from Hydro-Quebec into the northeastern United States. Loss of these facilities and the power supply from Quebec can have a substantial impact on power delivery systems in the northeastern portion of the United States. Within each Interconnection, power production and delivery systems are highly interdependent. In general, systems are operated such that the loss of one facility, or in some cases two or three facilities, will not cause cascading outages. Y2K poses the threat that common mode failures (such as all generator protection relays of a particular model failing simultaneously) or the coincident loss of multiple failures may result in stressing the electric system to the point of a cascading outage over a large area. This high level of interdependence within an Interconnection means that the robustness of the overall system needs to be tested against this new "contingency." An individualistic approach to the problem may not cover all potential problem areas (e.g., coordination with neighboring utilities) and, thus, could adversely affect operations within an Interconnection. An individual electric utility that invests tens of millions of dollars in solving Y2K problems could be affected in a major way by an outage initiated in neighboring systems that have not been as diligent. Therefore, preparation of the electricity power production and delivery systems in North America must be a coordinated team effort by those entities responsible for system reliability. All preventive programs do not have to be the same, but they do have to be coordinated. The industry will succeed or fail together in its readiness for Y2K.[16]

In today's networked world, no computer is an island, if we may be allowed a mix a few metaphors. Most computer systems are interdependent on other systems for at least part of their operations. For example, the global banking computer networks are each dependent on the accuracy of the information fed from one computer to

16 US Department of Energy NERC Report—The Y2K Coordination Plan for the Electricity Production and Delivery Systems of North America, June 12, 1998.

another. The Federal Reserve obtains its balance sheet, in part, from information received from member banks' computers. So, if the computer system at, say, a Chase Manhattan branch in Butte, Montana, is affected by the Y2K bug, it will ultimately affect the Fed's bottom line. For this illustration, we'll suppose the bank in Butte misread the new "00" to mean 1900, as noncompliant systems will do on 01/01/00, what will that mean locally? First, it will assume all its loans are 100 years overdue and apply interest accordingly. That will show up in the records as a huge negative balance. If your $70,000 mortgage remained unpaid for 100 years, with interest and penalties, it would be hundreds of millions of dollars in arrears—according to the computer. So, if the Butte branch had 700 such mortgages outstanding, the next computer report would subtract that figure from the bank's 31/12/99 balance. That figure would then be subtracted from the Fed's ledger. The operation would be repeated at every bank whose system succumbed to Y2K, and the Fed ledger would decrease exponentially. The Fed network then would send the incorrect data back out to the rest of the banking system computers, whose systems would also perform calculations based on incorrect data.

Garbage in—Garbage Out

+ + +

January 1, 2000, falls on a Saturday. Incorrect data will flow throughout the weekend, but the scope and extent of the damage won't be fully appreciated until the end of the next business day on Monday. Keep in mind that that is assuming that, unlike our Ryan family scenario, the power grid survives. If the power grid does go down, which is the most likely scenario at the time of this writing, then so will all of the banking computer systems that aren't on a fail-safe emergency backup system. Those with backup systems will continue to send and receive corrupted data that they will transmit to the "down" computers automatically when they come back on-line. This is a tiny example of how the *cascade effect* would work. It doesn't take into account what would happen if the telecommunications system went down, ending E-commerce entirely. Or if the satellite system went down, ending inter-bank communications of any kind, beyond some kind of Pony Express arrangement.

> The US Postal Service, long spoofed by technology wizards as the bastion of "snail mail," appears to be getting new respect from federal agencies and large companies drafting emergency computer backup plans for the Year 2000.

Worried that the so-called Millennium Bug could put at risk electronic transfers of data and money in some parts of the nation and abroad, private-sector and government groups are looking to the Postal Service as a backup delivery system if their computers malfunction, administration officials said.

Deputy Postmaster General Michael S. Coughlin, in an interview before departing for Hawaii to brief the postal Board of Governors, said the prospect of a mail surge in January 2000 is an "increasing concern."

The Postal Service has coped with floods, hurricanes, and earthquakes and found ways to move mail. It has even managed to absorb larger than expected volume, as it did during the United Parcel Service strike last year.[17]

In computer jargon there's a saying; "garbage in—garbage out." Computers are *binary*; that is, they operate on a high-speed version of an abacus.

---

17 "Postal Service Emerging As Key Year 2000 Backup," by Stephen Barr, *Washington Post* Staff Writer, Wednesday, October 7, 1998; page A19.

Electronic Prozac

+ + +

Everything you see on your Windows 95 desktop is the computer's interpretation of sequences of zeroes and ones. One zero out of place means that something won't work, but you won't know what it is until you try and use the affected device or program. Then the whole computer crashes, taking whatever operation it was working on at the time with it. Every element of your operating system is dependent upon the issuance of millions of instructions per second, coded into the combination sequences of those zeros and ones. If one of those millions of instructions per second is not issued, all subsequent instructions will be flawed, having assumed that all previous instructions had been carried out. The result is the electronic version of a nervous breakdown. Earlier we discussed the difference between Y2K *compliant* and Y2K *ready*. Being Y2K *ready* is analogous to giving Prozac to someone after their nervous breakdown has occurred. Y2K *compliant* is analogous to preventing the breakdown altogether. A patient on Prozac *seems* better than one who is not, but neither state is fully functional. It just takes the Prozac patient longer to fall apart once a little stress is applied. The same with computers. Once the nervous breakdown begins somewhere in the system, it will eventually break down entirely and crash.

The scenario the Tylers heard described by the UHF announcer of nuclear plant meltdowns, rioting in the streets, the collapse of transportation systems and runaway price gouging are not added for dramatic effect. As you will see as we go on, these nightmarish pictures could well be a glimpse into the near future.

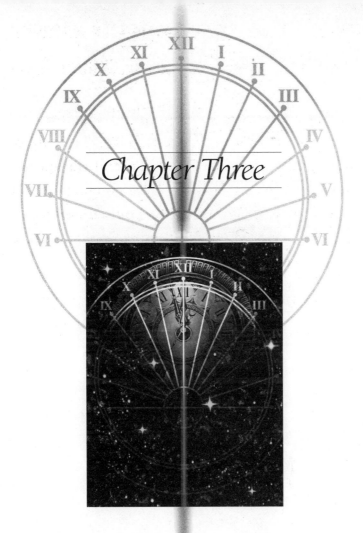

Chapter Three

t was good to finally be home. After nearly a week of two families living in the same room, everybody was getting cabin fever. Now that partial electrical service had been restored, the natural gas pumping stations were functioning, and, between the furnace and leaving the oven door open on the gas stove, the Tylers finally got the house warm enough to be comfortable.

Ryan and his brother were particularly close, and they enjoyed the week of enforced companionship. Once they settled into a routine, it took on the atmosphere of being on a camping trip. The brothers would chop wood, tinker in Roy's workshop, play cribbage by candlelight into the wee hours of the morning, and discuss the kinds of things that only brothers understand about each other. They had nowhere to go and nothing to do. So they just enjoyed it.

Not so with Val and her sister-in-law, Lorna. By Tuesday they were barely speaking. By Thursday they weren't speaking at all. Mikey and Kenny were getting along okay, but Roy's girls had returned to "normal" and the close proximity afforded no opportunity for them to get away from each other. It was bedlam.

On Friday morning, as another round of bick-
ering erupted over whose turn it was to get more
firewood, the power was restored. The lights
began to glow, dimly at first, but gradually they
grew stronger, almost like turning up a kerosene
lantern. The furnace kicked on, blowing icy cold
air throughout the house. For a moment, everyone sat in stunned silence, as if speaking would
break the spell and cause the miracle to evapo-
rate. Early on, both families had accepted the fact
that it might take weeks, or even months, before
the power grid went back on-line.

They sat for nearly a full minute, staring at the
flickering lamp on the end table. When it at last
glowed confidently, bathing the room with light,
both families let out a cheer. Roy ran to the front
door and threw it open. Around the neighborhood, he could see lights burning on back
porches. The sounds of cheering and laughter
could be heard coming from homes on either side.

Ryan had already turned on the television set
to try and get some information about what was
going on. The worst part of the blackout was that
nobody had any hard news. None of the network
stations were on the air, but the local UHF station
that had been the center of their lives for 30 minutes a day since the crisis began was back on the
job full time.

"Power has been partially restored for many
areas along the eastern seaboard this morning,
although there are still significant areas from
Maine to Virginia that are still blacked out. Even
those areas where power has been restored can
expect periodic brownout periods as the utility
companies struggle to develop a workable routine
that bypasses the Y2K programming failures. In
our area, programmers were able to temporarily
'trick' their mainframes to believe that it is 1972.
The year 1972 was the last calendar period that
coincides, date for date, with our current calendar. Officials warn that it is not foolproof and that
some areas may be subjected to additional periodic power blackouts until they work all the bugs
out. And they caution this is just a temporary
measure that only works in certain systems.

"We just happened to be lucky, folks. Our
area is served by hydro electricity generated by
Niagara Falls. Areas served by fossil fuel and
nuclear electrical generating plants remain dark
at this hour. Local telephone service has been
restored in a few areas, but long-distance carriers
are still down. WUTV is back on the air full time
for local broadcasting, but network satellite feeds
remain inoperable. Our news department is
working around the clock to try and put together
some kind of comprehensive newscast now that

we are at least partially in communication with other parts of the country, and we expect to be able to offer a more comprehensive report on the details and scope of what some are calling 'Disaster 2000.' In the meantime, here's what we already know . . ."

The lights dimmed, briefly, and when they came back up again, the television had lost the signal. Ryan turned it off.

An hour later, Roy pulled his pickup into their driveway. On the way home, they noticed that some neighborhoods remained dark while others seemed to have power. A few of the traffic signals were lit; others were dark. Those that were lit were cycling: green, yellow, red, green, yellow, red. They didn't know if they were among the fortunate neighborhoods until Ryan walked in the door and heard the furnace fan blowing. Roy helped them carry their things in, and they were alone, in their own home, for the first time in what seemed to be an eternity.

By now, they had learned that the Y2K had a global effect. Some areas fared better than others did, but the most industrialized nations suffered the greatest domestic disruption.

In Moscow, the Yeltsin government had been overthrown in a bloodless coup on Tuesday by ultra-nationalist politician Vladimir Zhirinovsky.

Upcoming national elections had been canceled, and the Russians were massing troops along the shared border with China. Russia, like the rest of the industrialized world, had been "logic-bombed" back into the 1940s. Russia's military arsenal of high-tech weapons was virtually useless. The Chinese, on the other hand, had a large stockpile of World War II vintage military hardware which they were now dusting off in anticipation of conflict with their neighbor to the north. The Millennium Bug had reversed the balance of power away from those nations whose arsenals were largely made up of "smart bombs" and toward less technically advanced nations like Iran, Syria, China, North Korea, and Cuba.

NORAD was rendered blind and helpless by the crash of the global computer network. The American high-tech arsenal of smart bombs was dependent on Global Positioning Satellites for guidance. The loss of the GPS Satellite system knocked out 90 percent of the US military arsenal, including our nuclear capability. The only defense we now had against attack was the fact that our principal enemies were as incapable of mounting an attack as we were at repelling one. Communication with American military bases abroad was nonexistent still, and there were rumors that a number of our bases had been nationalized by their host countries and our servicemen interned.

There were unconfirmed rumors of war in the Middle East, rioting continued in major cities around the world, and the rule of law had all but broken down in some areas. The TV announcer described it as "going to sleep in the 20th century and waking up in the Old West of the 1880s."

Can It Really Get *This* Bad?

+ + +

By now, you are probably thinking that we have gone "beyond the pale" in our fictional assessment of life after Millennial Midnight. Actually, we have "soft-pedaled" our story just a little, according to some experts. For example, limited electrical power has been restored somewhat more quickly in the Tylers' case than is likely for most of the country. The Tylers are located in a part of the country serviced by hydroelectricity provided by Niagara Falls. Hydroelectricity is somewhat different from fossil fuel or nuclear power. The energy necessary to create electric power is provided by the natural action of the waterfall, so it's already there; it only needs to be reharnessed. Those parts of the country that rely on fossil fuel or nuclear power will remain victims of the failed transportation system created by the power grid failure to begin with.

There are over 7,800 power supplying organizations in the United States. They are all tied together in one gigantic mainframe-controlled system that is laced with embedded chips. Sometimes power goes down all over a region. There are several regional districts. They are interconnected. Supposedly, the regional grids can be separated from the others if one goes down. But this circuit-breaker system, like everything else on the grids, relies on computers. Are you dependent on local public utilities that will go down if your local power generation system goes down? Yes, you are. You are TOTALLY dependent, in all likelihood. What if your local power system goes down with the regional system? Or even the national? What if your local system actually does get compliant but then is pulled into the black hole of the national power grid? Maybe it can pull out in time. Maybe the computers inside the region are all compliant as well as integrated. Don't count on it. It's not good enough to get a local system Y2K-compliant. Most of the power systems of the nation must be compliant or they will all go down, region by region, in one gigantic rolling blackout. If New York City goes down, Hog Jowls, Alabama, probably will, too. Then so does every computer in the country, compliant or not. And if they all go down, nobody will be able to repair any of them. There is no tomorrow if the national power grid goes down on January 1, 2000.[18]

There are dozens of major information "clusters" on the Internet that provide links and resources to articles and assessments of the Y2K bug's disruptive potential. Because the Internet is vastly unregulated and uncensored, it is a difficult task to separate the hysteria from the truth, but the sites and resources that we use throughout this book are widely respected voices within the Information Technology (IT) community. If the people who programmed, developed and maintain the global computer network don't know, then who does? And they say we can expect widespread power disruptions. Especially when it comes to just *how* to get the power grid on-line without the power necessary to reboot the computer network.

18 Y2K Internet Information site:
http://www.garynorth.com/y2k/results_.cfm/Power_Grid

Then there is nuclear power, which supplies about 20 percent of the power generated in the United States. What if the Nuclear Regulatory Commission closes nuclear plants in late 1999 because they are not Y2K compliant? At present, they are not compliant. The NRC has sent a warning to all 108 nuclear plants. Take 20 percent of the nation's power off-line in one day—40 percent in some regions—and what happens to the grid? The typical large city power plant has something in the range of 5,000 suppliers of goods and services. How will they be paid if the banks go down? Also, how will users pay the power companies? The grid may not go down overnight. (Then again, it may.) The problem is erosion, the second law of thermodynamics. Things wear out. How do they supply the plants with replacement parts if the banking system is in a crisis? This is the problem of the division of labor. A banking failure threatens the grid. The failure of the grid threatens everything. If your local power plant somehow solves these problems, what happens if others don't solve them? What if an overloaded grid shuts down? It could take down your local system. This is the coordination problem: among the local generation stations, among the regional grids, and among the suppliers.[19]

The Only Silver Bullets Belong to the Lone Ranger

+ + +

Programmers are trying out a number of "quick fixes" that can be used to "patch up" certain systems in the event of a Y2K failure. One of those temporary fixes that some experts are promoting is so simple that you wonder why nobody thought of it before. By resetting the system date to 1972, they argue, the computers will continue to function as if Millennial Midnight didn't happen. The 1972 calendar was identical in most respects to that of the Year 2000—it began on a Saturday and 1972 was a leap year. (Leap years occur every four years on the annual calendar, and every *400* years on the century calendar. For example, 1600 was a leap year; 1700 was not.) But it won't work as anything more than a temporary fix in closed systems, and then only in limited applications. Y2K is a threat because computers perform *time-based* calculations. One incorrect date is as useless as another. Garbage in, garbage out.

---

19   Y2K Internet Information site:
http://www.garynorth.com/y2k/results_.cfm/Power_Grid

The effect . . . if the fixing doesn't work, is a major collapse of key infrastructure: financial, telecom, transportation, utilities, food, water, health. During World War II the major infrastructure in every European country remained intact. Even with the collapse of the Soviet Union the major infrastructure of food, water, power, and transportation continued. We can also expect threats to cash, the paper value of wealth, and markets. The psychological and social consequences require some major acts of imagination to begin to get the picture of the consequences.[20]

The only "fix" that will work is the one that corporations and the government were reluctant to implement when there was still time. That fix is the individual examination of every line of code in every computer system by competent programmers and the manual correction of every line of faulty code discovered. If we had embarked on a crash program to repair the problem when it was first discovered, we *might* have gotten the job done on time, but at an estimated cost of from $680 *billion* to $3 *trillion*, depending on how you calculate it.

---

20 Douglas Carmichael, Y2K Week, Issue #6.

Instead, the decisionmakers preferred to ignore the warnings and place their bets on a silver bullet. Living in denial was much cheaper than putting out as much as $3 trillion as an investment whose return is exactly what you had before. Computers are working fine right now, went the reasoning, and eventually we'll come up with some kind of "catch-all" patch that will fix the problem. That's the "silver bullet" theory. But such a silver bullet would have to handle 15,000 IBM MVS mainframes, 40,000 IBM DOS/VSE midrange, 400,000+ IBM AS400s, 500,000+ DEC VAXs, Tandem, Wang, Xerox, Data General, Prime, Perkin-Elmer, and who knows how many other manufacturers.

All are different platforms, most are written in different languages, all have different source codes, most are custom programmed, and very few still have the original documentation to work from. Sadly, there *is* no silver bullet.

First of all, while COBOL programs are the main culprits, they're by no means the only ones. Every application—in every imaginable programming language—must be checked for two-digit dates. It's impossible for a single tool to do this. More insidiously, many programmers did not label date fields logically—or at all. An automated tool cannot possibly catch every single date field when there is no single method that everyone uses to label them.

Even date fields that have obvious labels might not be formatted in the same way. Does the day come before or after the month? Does the two-digit year *40* represent the year that a building was constructed (1840), a birthdate (1940), or an insurance policy's expiration date (2040)? Cases like these make it obvious that human logic will have to be involved.[21]

What About Bill Gates?

+ + +

Many of those who are betting their future on a "silver bullet" are looking to Bill Gates and Microsoft for the recipe. How many times have you heard somebody say something like; "I'll let Bill Gates worry about it," or, "Microsoft will figure out something," or some other such nonsense? Well, it ain't gonna happen, folks. With all the technical expertise at their disposal, working on software systems that *they themselves developed,* <u>knowing that Y2K threatens their very existence</u>, Microsoft was at least able to bring its own software into

---

21 C|NET, "8 Myths About the Millennium Bug."

compliance. All of Microsoft's new operating systems, like Windows98, is Y2K compliant <u>now</u>—it says so right on the box! It only makes sense, then, if Microsoft can make *its* software compliant, the same principles should be adaptable to fix other software platforms, right?

It would seem so, on the surface. But, the truth is, Microsoft is Year 2000 compliant, but 2001 is going to be a real problem.

For example, while 96 percent of Microsoft's software was either Y2K "compliant" or "compliant with minor issues," the BIOS chips in some PCs meant that Microsoft's Y2K solution would only work for a year and would break again in 2001. The BIOS chip provides the interface between a PC's central processing chip (such as the Pentium II chip) and the PC's "real-time clock," which contains a quartz chip. While PC real-time clocks are Y2K compliant nowadays, most BIOS chips are not and will strip the year field of a date back to two characters ("00" instead of "2000") before handing it onto the operating system. Microsoft had fixed this problem in its operating systems but, for BIOS chips that reset each time the computer was switched off, the fix would only last a year since the fix only applied to the year

"00" and not "01," Microsoft Year 2000 strategy manager Mr. Jason Matusow said.[22]

In other words, Microsoft the [Y2K] Giant Slayer has failed! Although they have developed a software "fix," *it doesn't really work!* Instead, it's a "workaround" patch. If Microsoft, with all its billions of dollars, programming resources, and its own self interest driving the whole project, can't come up with a workable fix, what does that say about the "silver bullet option" as a whole?

A World Without Telephones

+ + +

Sometimes it almost sounds idyllic—a world without telephones, fax machines, pagers and cell phones. As the Ryan brothers discovered, it does seem to have its advantages. But so does playing hooky from work—until payday, that is. And the "payday" from all this peace and quiet is that there is no payday. Without telecommunications, there are no ATM's, bank wire transfers, credit card sales, debit card sales, or check verification terminals. The only cash available is whatever you have on hand at Millennial Midnight. When it's gone, it's gone, and it could take all you have just to buy a loaf of bread. But how likely is

22 *Australian Financial Review*, August 20, 1998.

it that the global telephone network will suffer a catastrophic breakdown?

"Reliable telecommunications services are made possible by a complex web of highly interconnected networks supported by national and local carriers and service providers, equipment manufacturers and suppliers, and customers. The key is interoperability: all of the pieces must work together."[23]

Unless all the pieces do work together, the system will not work beyond December 31, 1999, according to the sworn testimony made following a GAO investigation of the Federal Communications Commission's Y2K readiness. And the GAO has serious doubts that it will.

"Underlying weaknesses in FAA's management have allowed the agency's Year 2000 computer security and other information technology problems to persist. Our work over the last two years has identified some of the root causes of, and pinpointed solutions to, these long-standing problems—including an incomplete systems

---

23 GAO Congressional testimony of Joel C. Willemssen, Director, Civil Agencies Information Systems, Accounting and Information Management Division.

architecture, weak software acquisition capabilities, unreliable cost information, and a problematic organizational culture. Although FAA has initiated efforts in response to some of our recommendations on these issues, *most of them have not been fully implemented*"[24] [emphasis ours].

One of the world's largest telecommunications giants, Motorola, is suffering "sticker shock" over the repairs necessary to enable it to remain on-line through the millennium. Despite the enormous costs, the phone lines may still go dead on New Year's Day 2000.

Motorola said about $150 million of the total estimated future costs relate to internal resources. External costs through September 26, 1998, were about $70 million. "The company has and will continue to devote substantial resources to address its Year 2000 issues," Motorola said in the filing. Motorola said, however, it cannot be sure that neither its nor its suppliers' products do not contain undetected Year 2000 problems.[25]

---

24 GAO Congressional testimony of Joel C. Willemssen, Director, Civil Agencies Information Systems, Accounting and Information Management Division.
25 "Motorola to Spend $290-$340 Mln on Y2K Bug," *Reuters*, November 13, 1998.

A Millennium War?

+ + +

The telecommunications blackout will do much more than shut down the global economy, as if that weren't bad enough. We live in the Information Age, and the rapid exchange of information is the foundation upon which the global political infrastructure rests.

We've already had a couple of foretastes of what Y2K is capable of, even though most people weren't aware of the Year 2000 connection. In April 1998 a "software problem" caused a cascade failure within their systems. Before it could be contained, 44 hubs were knocked out of service. This cut off phone service to vast numbers of both business and residential telephone customers. Certain business functions were immediately crippled; email services, banking transfers, manufacturing orders, ATM machines, and credit card services were compromised. AT&T explained that a software-generated problem which began in two of their frame relay switches replicated itself into some 145 nodes across the frame relay network. Phone service in the affected areas was out for up to 20 hours. Since AT&T handles about 40 percent of American network customers, this was a major problem that cost American business multiple billions of dollars. Although the blackout was limited to AT&T networks, to those people directly affected it might as well have knocked out the entire globe. And it only lasted a day. What effect would it have had if the problem had lasted days, weeks, or even months?

In our story, the legitimate government of Russia falls victim to a bloodless coup d'etat. Such a coup would be possible during an information blackout. The sequestering of information is the classic tactic of a dictatorship. The attempted coup against Gorbachev that eventually propelled Yeltsin to power was conducted against the backdrop of a news blackout.

Y2K will reach well beyond the limits of the earth's atmosphere. Orbiting in outer space is a network of communications satellites that digitally bounce transmission signals from one place on the planet to another. That is what provides CNN and virtually every other network with the kind of instant communication we have come to depend on. When the computer grid goes down, so will the satellite grid.

It is not far-fetched to believe that many nations will seek redress for wrongs, real or imagined, committed against them by technologically superior enemies while under the cover of electronic "darkness." It would be naive to believe that the Arab nations would not immediately press the military advantage they would suddenly enjoy over Israel's technology-dependent military forces.

With military heads buried so firmly in the sands of time, the risks are becoming ever more disturbing. Could the result be a Millennium War? . . . A US submarine or fighter aircraft depends on hundreds of thousands of chips, and the systems that command such weapons use more than a million. Complex systems are a bug hunter's nightmare. Israel has just realized that it will have no effective air defense on January 1, 2000, unless the native computer talent is mobilized rapidly. In one of the great post-Cold War ironies, the US is spending millions of dollars to help Russia ensure it has a working air defense system. There is already plenty of evidence after the end of the Cold War on how Russia's decaying defense establishment may result in the launch of even its nuclear arsenal, because of mistakes in its air defense and command and control systems. The US and Britain are beginning to fret that by having to make rapid adjustments and by using foreign computer programmers such as in India to repair these problems, the result may be seriously compromised reliability and security of weapons systems. And as the modern armed forces of the US and Britain "war game" the Y2K problem, they are growing more worried about military contingencies that result from economic collapse. East Asia's economic meltdown reminded them that riots, as we saw on the streets of Jakarta, can get out of control quickly when panicked people think their money is worthless. There are also serious concerns about how the collapse of vulnerable public utilities may cause emergencies that require military assistance.[26]

The NORAD Test

+ + +

Back in 1993, the North American Air Defense Command conducted a secret Y2K compliance test. They wanted see what would happen to all their computers, the ones that warn of a nuclear attack, on New Year's Day of the Year 2000. They moved ahead the dates to just before midnight of the dreaded day and waited. According to a story in the *Boston Globe,* everything froze. Everything. For the duration of the test, the United States was

---

26 *The Singapore Straits Times,* August 10, 1998. *Note:* The writer is Gerald Segal, Director of Studies, at the International Institute for Strategic Studies.

completely blind to attack. That's why it was conducted in secret. It took days to get everything back on-line, even though all they had to do was move the clock back. But once they did, every system had to be re-booted and reset and incorrect date stamps had to be located and fixed.

The problem goes way beyond NORAD. If the problem isn't fixed, it will affect everything from nuclear missiles to a sergeant's battlefield laptop. All the various satellites, sensors, radars, and communications networks that link them into a unified fighting machine are also vulnerable to shutdown. The *Globe* carried this chilling quote from its June 21, 1998, edition. "The Year 2000 problem is the electronic equivalent of El Nino," Deputy Defense Secretary John J. Hamre told the Senate Armed Services Committee. "This is going to have implications in the world . . . that we can't even comprehend." Hamre said the situation is so grim that the Pentagon is developing a program to share data from US early-warning satellites with other countries. That includes Russia and China. Otherwise, come 2000, such nations may find themselves in the dark, uncertain whether an attack is coming or not. In a crisis, that could provoke an accidental launch. In fact, the date glitch itself is enough to spark an automatic launch at some of the world's nuclear missile sites. India and Pakistan are teetering on the brink of nuclear war. Their computer systems are among the least prepared for Y2K. It wouldn't take much for one side or the other to push the nuclear button.

Smart Bombs Get Stupid

+ + +

During the Gulf War, the United States proudly pointed to the successes of our smart weapons systems. You'll remember the footage of bombs being directed into windows or down chimneys during air attacks over Baghdad. Back then, only 10 percent of our arsenal was in the so-called smart bomb category. Following the war, we set out to upgrade all our weapons systems. The Pentagon developed weapons that followed the Global Positioning System, or GPS. The GPS breaks down the planet into small grid coordinates. Weapons can be guided to those coordinates using information from GPS satellites orbiting the earth. Both the weapons and the GPS guidance systems are operated by computer systems and embedded chips. In the event of a catastrophic Y2K failure, those weapons systems will downgrade from smart to so stupid they won't even fire. Think of the potential. The world's great superpower blinded by the failure of NORAD's early warning system. Our awesome arsenal will be useless. All we will have left is our conventional forces and conventional weapons. The most powerful military nations will be those who rely on World War II military technology. One military analyst predicted that a complete Y2K failure would put the US on a military par with countries like North Korea, Yugoslavia, or Cuba.[27]

27 Cliff Ford, *The International Intelligence Briefing Special Report* "Counting Down to Millennial Midnight."

Chapter Four

Monday, January 10, 2000

arly in the crisis, Ryan had welcomed the arrival of the National Guard troops dispatched by FEMA as a symbol that the country was still intact. Having armed troops roaming the streets was unsettling to his family, but Ryan was an ex-Marine who initially viewed them as comrades-in-arms.

The troops were ordered in under Presidential Directive #63, which gave the Federal Emergency Management Authority total control of communications, law enforcement, the utility industry, and the unrestricted use of federal troops to enforce martial law. Under the martial law declaration, all civil liberties were suspended. Citizens were subject to arrest without warrant and could be held without bail for up to 30 days without the necessity of filing formal charges. Anyone caught outside after curfew was subject to arrest. People began vanishing without a trace.

Newsgathering organizations were now required to submit their copy to FEMA censors before being broadcast. Broadcasting uncensored material was declared to be an act of treason. As a result, news programs were little more than infomercials proclaiming the latest FEMA regulations.

Local newspapers were ordered closed, and *USAToday* was "temporarily" nationalized and proclaimed the "official voice" of the United States government. The paper was distributed nationally. A slender "regional" section was inserted that gave heavily censored state and local information. All the articles in both sections were filled with soothing milquetoast about how things would return to normal "soon" and that everything was under control. The government was functioning normally, the paper said. This is just a temporary state of emergency, and the dictatorial powers wielded by FEMA and its agencies are to "help us cope with a difficult time."

The "difficult time" came for Ryan Tyler on Saturday, January 7, 2000, exactly one week after he woke up freezing in the dark, and only two weeks after his family celebrated Christmas in the 20th century—before Y2K.

Supermarket shelves had been stripped bare by Day Two of Y2K. The transportation systems were still not operating, and what little food made its way to the northern states by way of FEMA was carefully rationed. Each head of household could draw a seven-day supply of MRE's (military Meals, Ready to Eat) for each member of the family. The dehydrated military rations had a shelf life measured in years. Each meal was carefully balanced for maximum nutrition, rather than flavor, but they weren't that bad. Although his brother Roy had already laid in a three-month supply of MRE's, the crisis looked like it would last forever, so both brothers went down to the FEMA distribution center to claim their share.

As they were heading back to Ryan's house, Ryan spotted smoke coming from his neighborhood. They arrived to find most of the block in flames. Ryan's house was gone. So were Val and Mikey. He never saw either of them again. He never found out what happened to them.

He remembered, bitterly, the so-called "experts" who had made a living during the last year of the 20th century debunking the "Y2K doomsayers," claiming the Millennium Bug was "over-hyped nonsense." At the time, it was easy enough to believe.

Ryan realized how much he had taken for granted all his adult life. Ryan had lived a fairy tale existence all his life without ever being aware of it. He had never heard a shot fired in anger. He had never known hunger, cold, or homelessness. All his life he only needed to flip a switch to obtain warmth and light. He could jump into his car and drive to the nearest supermarket where the bounty of an entire nation was neatly arranged for the taking.

Over a period of just 10 days, Ryan lost everything he had accumulated over the course of a lifetime, including his family. It may have been a "temporary emergency" as far as the government was concerned, but Ryan's loss was as permanent as anything could possibly be. And if anything about Y2K was "over-hyped" it was the rhetoric of the morons who downplayed the possibility of catastrophe, back while there was still time to prepare.

Joe Everyman
+ + +

Sometimes it just isn't enough to think of things in abstract terms. Sure, we all *know* what happens when we turn on a light switch. The lights come on. And when we turn it on and the lights *don't* come on, we weigh the options according to our experience. The bulb is burned out. Or a fuse blew. Or, rarely, there is a temporary service interruption, following a severe storm or an accident of some kind. But in every instance, the operative word is *temporary*. The light won't come on until we change the bulb, or replace the fuse, or, in the worst case scenario, until after the storm passes, or, after the utility pole or downed line is replaced. But we *know* based on our experience that the light will *eventually* come back on. Thinking of it in terms of weeks, months, or even years is not part of our mind-set. It is just too foreign a thought for the consequences to fully register in our minds.[28]

That is one reason that we decided to personalize it in some small way by sharing the experience of Joe Everyman—Ryan Tyler in this instance—so that each of us can understand that we could well share the same experience, or worse, in the event of a Y2K disaster. We made a point of minimizing the impact, believe it or not. Limited electricity and telephone service was restored relatively early on in our story. If the power grid *does* go down, utilities may not be restored for months or even years!

When we were researching this book, we tried to find a credible source arguing that the Y2K will not have a major impact of some kind on modern society if all necessary repairs aren't made in time. There are hundreds of information technology experts, from Ed Yardeni,[29] Chief Economist

---

28 "Telling the public that the computers can't do arithmetic and they face imminent danger is such an abstract concept that most do not take it seriously." *Testimony of IT professional Alan Simpson before Congress, June 1998.*
29 Dr. Yardeni is the Chief Economist and a Managing Director of Deutsche Bank Securities (North America). Working from the firm's headquarters in New York City, he writes the *Global Economic Analysis, Global Portfolio Strategy, Global Economic Briefing,* and *Y2K Reporter,* as well as a variety of topical studies. In these publications, Dr. Yardeni explores issues and trends in the economy and financial markets that are vital to a broad spectrum of decision-makers. Dr. Yardeni previously served as Chief Economist for C.J. Lawrence, Prudential Securities, and E.F. Hutton. He taught

for Deutsche Morgan Grenville, to John Hamre,[30]
US Assistant Secretary of Defense, all warning of
a coming Y2K catastrophe. Finding someone
willing to lay his reputation on the line by saying
Y2K will have no impact is quite a bit harder.

> According to the experts and observers
> following the fix that's now underway, the
> "Millennium Bug" will bring anything
> from a few bumps in the road to
> Armageddon 2000. On one extreme are an
> assorted lot—anticipating global short-
> ages, famine, social turbulence and eco-
> nomic hard times—who have already
> begun preparing for the worst. On the
> other are those confident that the patch-
> up job will work with at most a few short-
> comings, perhaps the equivalent of an
> extra natural disaster or two in the earth's
> near future.[31]

------

at Columbia University's Graduate School of Business and
was an economist with the Federal Reserve Bank of New
York. He also held positions at the Federal Reserve Board   of
Governors and the US Treasury Department in Washington,
DC. *Source: Deutsche Bank Securities.*
30 "The Year 2000 problem is the electronic equivalent of El
Nino," Deputy Defense Secretary John J. Hamre told the Senate
Armed Services Committee. "This is going to have implica-
tions in the world . . . that we can't even comprehend." *Source:
Boston Globe, June 21, 1998 [see Chapter Three for context].*
31 "Y2K: What happens when the computers go hay-
wire?" Mark K. Anderson, *The Valley Advocate* 07/09/98.

As this article points out, there are basically *two* groups of experts, those who predict catastrophe and those who predict something less. There are no credible spokespersons for the view that Y2K will have no effect at all.

20th Century Toys
or 21st Century Junk?

+ + +

Try, for a moment, to think of all the labor saving devices that will vanish at the stroke of midnight, barring some kind of programming miracle. Stop right now, where you are, and look around. Make a list of just how many devices are within sight of you right now that require electricity to operate. Come January 1, 2000, all that you have listed will be just so much junk. Come January 10, there isn't a single item on your list you wouldn't trade for a $20 bag of groceries, in 20th century terms. Who knows what a bag of groceries will cost 10 days after the power and transportation grids go black and the phones go dead?

> To run a phone system, one needs a stable power source. But the continued, uninterrupted flow of electricity is not a sure thing when the millennial date change comes. Senator Christopher Dodd of Connecticut expressed his dismay about

this problem last month when the Senate's committee on Y2K learned that only two of the 10 major utilities it had spoken with had even completed their assessment of the situation. "We're no longer at the point of asking whether or not there will be any power disruptions," Dodd said, "but we are now forced to ask how severe the disruptions are going to be." Simpson continued that thought. "Without power and without a stable power source, we won't have telecommunications," he said. "If we don't have telecommunications, we won't have power. The power stations use the telecommunications for command and control. It's a loop. You could get a big cascading effect, and that's one of the big fears about what's going to happen."One recent harbinger of danger on the horizon was a February power outage in Auckland, New Zealand, that was unrelated to Y2K. Power cables leading into the city failed, and according to Reuters, the resulting power loss "crippled the hub of the nation's business community." Some residents' water and sewage systems stopped working. All activity but essential services came to a standstill. Students locked out of their

dormitories had to camp out in the suburbs. The Auckland incident shifted many
Y2K observers' outlook on the prospects
for a clean fix. "I would be less pessimistic
had I not seen Auckland," Simpson said.
"It took them six weeks to get normality
returned in one city. And they had the rest
of the nation running perfectly normally.
All the backup generators burned out in
12 hours. That was a real wake-up call that
no one here has even heard of. That made
me realize how ill-prepared we are."[32]

Don't Look to Washington

+ + +

Despite the emphasis the Clinton administration
placed on Information Technology during the
1996 election, the White House refused to admit
the full extent of the danger posed by Y2K until
there was no way to sweep it under the rug any
longer. One of the most respected Y2K experts in
America is John Westergaard. On July 6, 1998, he
gave testimony before the Senate subcommittee
that was charged with examining the Year 2000
computer problem.

---

32 "Y2K: What happens when the computers go haywire?" Mark K. Anderson, *The Valley Advocate* 07/09/98.

Senator Moynihan advised the President of Y2K by letter in July 1996 and recommended appointment of a "Manhattan Project" style Y2K Czar to direct federal compliance. A perfunctory response was received in November, not directly from the President but from Frank Raines at OMB. The Senator then arranged a meeting with Secretary of the Treasury Bob Rubin and Assistant Secretary Larry Summers on December 14, 1996, in which I participated. Rubin and Summers were generally aware of the problem. We learned that Treasury was then budgeting circa $75 million for Y2K. According to a recent report, the figure in just 15 months has blossomed to $800 million. The first public acknowledgment of Y2K by the White House occurred on August 15, 1997, a full year after the Moynihan letter, when the President stated at a press conference that <u>Americans need not worry about the "computer clock" problem</u>.

Now, if the problem is as severe as we sincerely believe it to be, how dare we contradict the President of the United States when he tells us not to "worry about the computer clock problem"? Ryan Tyler, and millions more like him,

believed the President's assurances and gambled
their future on them. Does the White House
know something the rest of us don't? Or is the
White House playing politics with your future?

> What has the administration's technology
> point man, Vice President Al Gore, been
> doing for the last five years? . . . At its core,
> this is not a technology crisis, it's a leader-
> ship crisis. Distracted by scandals and side-
> tracked by questionable crises like global
> warming, the Clinton-Gore administration
> is failing to ensure that vital government
> computers will be fixed in time. Nor are
> they impressing the American public and
> foreign governments with the urgency of
> this crisis. Why such silence? Are they try-
> ing to limit public concern until after the
> mid-term elections? The stakes are too
> high for such partisan political games.[33]

When the crisis does hit, the White House has
already made all the contingency plans it needs.
Through a series of Executive Orders and Presidential Directives, the Federal Emergency Management Authority [FEMA] is empowered with
sweeping dictatorial powers[34] not unlike those that

---

33 Testimony of Steve Forbes, May 13, in a memorandum
to Congress.
34 See endnotes.

Ryan Tyler found so restrictive. When the lights go out, they'll be on the job. But it can be argued that, if the White House had taken the crisis seriously at the outset, there might have been time to prevent the lights from going out at all.

But the Government Says Not to Worry

+ + +

To inform the public of the real threats would actually cause many of those threats to unfold. It's classic panic psychology. If you tell people "corn supplies are critically low," they will run out and buy corn to avoid the shortage. This behavior will <u>cause</u> the corn shortage to worsen, creating a self-fulfilling prophecy.

The same applies to financial institutions. If you warn people that their deposits might be threatened, they'll take their money out. Doing that will <u>cause</u> the bank runs, worsening the threat to deposits.

For this reason, the public cannot be—and won't be—told the truth. No public official can possibly acknowledge the validity of this statement without simultaneously violating it.

We believe there is a planned policy of disinformation regarding the real Y2K threat. Most government officials are taking up the mantra of Sally Katzen of the GAO when she said, "Hey, everything is fine!" You hear this from the FAA, Social Security, the IRS, Medicare, and even the Dept. of Defense. Yet we continue to see admissions that those statements really aren't true.[35]

The government really *can't* tell the public the whole truth! The Rodney King riots in LA are just one example of what people will do when they share a common, amplified emotion. If anger can cause people to burn down their own neighborhoods, pull innocent victims from their vehicles and beat them to death, and unleash lethal firearms attacks on firemen trying to save their homes, what will unbridled <u>fear</u> cause if the people are told their world is on the verge of total collapse?

---

35 As stated in the DCAIS-AIMD-GAO-SGMIT-GRO report: "OMB's assessment of the current status of federal Year 2000 progress is predominantly based on agency reports that have not been consistently reviewed or verified. Without independent reviews, OMB and the President's Council on Year 2000 Conversion have little assurance that they are receiving accurate information. In fact, we have found cases in which agencies' systems compliance status as reported to OMB has been inaccurate. For example, the DOD Inspector General estimated that almost three quarters of DOD's mission-critical systems reported as compliant in November 1997 had not been certified as compliant by DOD components. In May 1998, the Department of Agriculture reported 15 systems as compliant, even though these were replacement systems that were still under development or were planned for development. (The department removed these systems from compliant status in its August 1998 quarterly report.)"

Chapter Five

THE PRE-
MILLENNIUM BUG

The Beeper Blackout

+ + +

n our story, Ryan hasn't a clue about the Y2K bug. In reality, if predictions hold true, he will probably have already experienced enough Y2K interruptions to have given him at least a passing acquaintance with the term, if not a working knowledge of its hazards.

At the time of this writing, we have already been given several glimpses into the kind of havoc that will be routine come Millennial Midnight. On May 19, 1998, an onboard processor on Galaxy 4, one of the communications satellites orbiting the earth, failed, silencing 85 percent of the country's pagers at one blow. Hospitals were unable to reach doctors, key government officials were suddenly out of touch, and millions of lives were disrupted. There were isolated cellular service interruptions. Telecommunications disruption shut down the majority of ATM machines and other electronic business like bank wire transfers were affected. The blackout lasted less than 24 hours. The cost to business was estimated in the tens of billions of dollars. Since Galaxy 4's backup processor had failed the year before, the multi-billion-dollar PanAmSat satellite became so much more orbiting space junk.

In the summer of 1998, four more satellites belonging to Hughes Electronics Corp. failed over a two-month period. Hughes' corporate reputation was impressive; they had gone 35 years without a single operational failure. But over the period of June-July 1998, *four more* of them stopped working! Of the 82 satellites that are currently orbiting the earth, 35 of them are of the same design as the five that failed. Hughes engineers don't know why the embedded processor failed, but they were unable to rule out a date-sensitive miscalculation. Whether these failures are related to hardware or an early sensitivity to Y2K is less important to the purpose of this book than is the affect the failures had across the board, touching almost every American in some way. Hughes Corporation's engineers were satisfied it was the failure of a single embedded processor that shut down the whole system. The *cascade effect* brought much of the nation's business to a complete standstill until switching to other satellites in similar orbits restored service. What will happen if there are no satellites to transfer these functions to, come January 1, 2000?

In God We Trust, Others Pay Cash

✦ ✦ ✦

As long as the phantom money exists electronically, people trust the system. So they keep making deposits. If the banking computer system fails, a panic inevitably follows. People will begin to demand their deposits back—in cash. Banks will be forced to call in the outstanding loans to meet demand. Those who can't foreclose quickly enough will fail. Our entire economy is based on the fiction that there is enough money to go around. A worldwide computer collapse will expose the fractional reserve system as the pyramid scheme it actually is. But even if the banking system computers survive, that's no guarantee the economy will. Charles Schwab Corp., the largest US discount broker, said its internal computer system failed for two hours on April 13, 1998. The failure halted trades, broker access to accounts, and customers' ability to buy and sell stocks over the Internet. Schwab has 1.5 million active on-line accounts. A company spokesman said the failure occurred in Schwab's primary data center in Phoenix, Arizona. It affected not just on-line trading, but telephone trades because brokers couldn't access customer accounts. Suppose a large number of small- and medium-sized businesses can't communicate with the banking system because their computers fail? Those businesses will have to turn to cash. That would be enough to unwind the whole fractional reserve debt pyramid. Even if all the banks are 100 percent compliant. Remember, all that holds the fractional reserve system together is public confidence.

Federal Reserve notes are not *money*. Money is what people will accept in exchange for goods and services. If electronic funds transfers are unreliable, people will revert to other traditional forms of currency like gold and silver coins or trade goods like food, gasoline or other basic necessities.

The Pre-Millennium Bug(s)

+ + +

By the time Ryan Tyler's story begins, most of us will already have become acquainted with what might be called "pre-millennium" bugs that are also sensitive to the coming century date change. The closer we get to Year 2000, the more aware we will become. Calculations that project into the next century have already caused credit cards bearing expiration dates ending in double zeroes to be recalled. Insurance policies, mortgages and other forward looking, date sensitive instruments have already run into problems in isolated instances. It will only get worse as more and more of these calculations look forward past the century mark.

One recent example of the date recognition flaw that gives us a little taste of the kind of confusion we can expect to see becoming more common as we approach the century mark happened in the international banking capital in Switzerland.

> A millennium-style bug has struck early for a Swiss pensioner, who received a letter ordering him to attend elementary school. The 105-year-old retired teacher received the letter as his local town hall's database only listed the birthdate of its residents by the last two digits, thus calculating him to be only five years old.[36]

01/01/99—Let the Testing Begin!

+ + +

One of the most important aspects of Y2K preparation is the testing phase. On the first of January, 1999, that phase is scheduled to begin for computer network systems across the globe. Testing is a critical phase in the Y2K compliance operation. Once the faulty date code has been rewritten to accommodate the century date, it will take a full year of operational testing to hunt down and kill the various bugs that rewriting the source code will inevitably create. If these bugs aren't squashed in time, they will cascade through the global computer networks, fouling data and disrupting systems that remain operational after

---

36 VNU Business Publications, November 5, 1998.

Millennial Midnight, in effect, nullifying the upgrades already in place.

The Waiting Game
+ + +

Come Millennial Midnight, it is a waiting game. Systems that haven't been repaired will send contaminated data to systems that have. That data, with its date and time stamps intact, will interact with the upgraded system. The result of the contaminated data passing through the system will be the same as if both systems were not compliant. The "garbage in, garbage out" equation applies here.

Think of it like a simple math equation. If you change one part of the formula, no matter how slight, it will change the answer. Take a 30-year mortgage, for example. It will be paid off at a specific date. But if you miss a payment, especially early in the mortgage, it changes the payoff date, by years if the missed payment was early enough. All we did was change one number in an equation. Years of payments are added as a result.

If the computer thinks you've missed every payment made after 1900, how much do you owe on your mortgage? When will it be paid off?

Gee, Thanks!
+ + +

If a Smith-Barney investor had known exactly

when to make the withdrawal, he would have made a killing. You remember Smith-Barney? They "make money the old fashioned way; they earn it," according to their commercials. Well, the Smith-Barney brokerage house thought they had their computers fixed. Their programmers tried to expand the date formula to eight digits by putting a nineteen in front. It worked on several dry runs. Then they tried a live test. They fired up their computer systems, and everything started humming just fine. Soon after, some of their customers called to thank them for the good job they were doing handling their investments. They checked and found the computer had added $19 million to each of their customers' accounts. Smith-Barney has 525,000 accounts. The total error exceeded $10 trillion. That's more than twice the national debt.

Remember, that is just *one* investment banking firm. Multiply that times the number of investment firms on Wall Street, and you have a small picture of the potential damage. In the Smith-Barney case, they were lucky. Had their computers connected with outside computers on the network, the problem could have cascaded to them. That would have brought on the millennium catastrophe early. It also shows how vulnerable the whole economic system is. Edward

Yardeni put it this way. "Everyone said the Titanic was the wonder of the age back then, and it was. This [Y2K] is Titanic America."

Will We Make It?

+ + +

According to the Gartner Group, some 80 percent of the infrastructure providers (utilities, etc.) and global business giants that had announced they would begin testing on 01/01/99 will miss their appointment. They started too late, allocated too little for repairs, and don't have sufficient manpower to meet the deadline. Business planning systems will break down as they attempt to assess future projects through 01/01/00. January 1, 1999, is the target date for the new European currency to go on-line. Preparing for that change has overwhelmed programming talent that otherwise might have been occupied preparing for the Y2K bug.

According to *Jane's Defense Weekly*, the US Defense Department has admitted it is far behind in the drive to prepare for Y2K. Defense Secretary William Cohen said, "The DOD is making insufficient progress in its efforts to solve its Y2K computer problem." Cohen requested detailed reports and other actions from all branches of the Pentagon, including overseas commands, weapons programs and data centers, to improve accountability for corrective actions.

The DOD plans to spend an estimated $2 billion to fix and test thousands of computer systems, many of them deemed "mission-critical," to ensure they can compute the date change from 1999 to 2000 without affecting operations. Cohen singled out several areas for special attention, including the nuclear command and control system and all major weapons programs.

> Recently, an undisclosed DOD source indicated that the DOD had been trying to run simulated programs on nuclear missile silo computers to see what would happen on January 1, 2000. In short, there was a total breakdown of the fail-safe protection. Some missiles shut down entirely. Others fired their missiles. Other DOD sources have reported that missiles in silos armed with nuclear warheads may self-destruct in the silo.[37]

In our story, that is what happened to Saddam Hussein's missile attack against Israel. It was fun to let Israel "win one" for a change, but our story

37 *The McIlvaney Intelligence Advisor,* P.O. Box 84904, Phoenix, Arizona 85071, September '98.

is just fiction based on the best available intelligence. That same intelligence says it could just as easily be *our* nuclear arsenal shutting down, detonating on launch, or, missing targets altogether.

01/04/99
+ + +

April 1, 1999, is the beginning of the fiscal year for some jurisdictions. Canada begins its fiscal year April 1. So does Japan. In the United States, April 1 marks New York State's fiscal new year. Rolling over into the new fiscal year necessarily means that these jurisdictions will conduct planning past the century date through 01/04/00.

A Millennium Bug glitch in New York will make the front pages of newspapers around the world.

> Nearly 60 percent of the state's towns, villages, cities, counties, and fire districts responded to the survey, which was mailed out in March. And according to the results, compiled over the past six weeks, the majority of New York's noncounty local governments aren't prepared to cope with potentially devastating computer problems that may strike on January 1, 2000.

> A breakdown showed that 26 percent of the state's cities, 54 percent of towns, 48 percent of villages, and 61 percent of fire

districts have yet to make plans to deal with the year 2000 problem, McCall said.

"The consequences of failing to face the year 2000 problem are extraordinary," McCall said in a statement. He called on local officials to check and recheck vital systems responsible for operations such as jail security, 911 emergencies and traffic lights to ensure a smooth transition into the next millennium.[38]

A Japanese collapse could be the straw that breaks the back of the global economy. After April 1, 1999, Japan may be forced to admit its systems won't make it across the century mark. The stock market will react by pulling its remaining investments out of Japan. If Japan were to retaliate by converting their US investments into cash, the US economy would be shattered. America is the world's largest debtor nation. Japan is the world's largest creditor nation. Most of Japan's credit is in the form of US instruments of debt, the second largest concentration of US debt on earth.

---

38 "Study Eyes New York's Readiness," *Online News,* September 11, 1998. http://www.computerworld.com/home/news.nsf/all/9809115nystate

01/07/99

+ + +

Forty-four US states launch their new fiscal years on July 1, 1999. The problems experienced in New York in April will now be felt across the nation. The global nature of Y2K and the cascade effect of multiple systems failures will impact the national consciousness for the first time. Many states have admitted that they lack the time and the money to fix all the Y2K related problems in time for July 1, let alone make the fail-safe testing deadline of July 1, 1999. We will probably start to see widespread public panic as the local infrastructure is affected. We can expect to see the beginnings of a mass migration as people start abandoning the big cities for safer rural communities. Interstates will be jammed with traffic, and in many states, automated traffic controls could be inoperable or unreliable.

22/08/99

+ + +

Following our successes in the Gulf War, the Pentagon embarked on an all-out campaign to upgrade America's "smart weapons" arsenal. Operation Desert Storm was a perfect proving ground for the current crop of laser-guided smart bombs. Pentagon planners were able to identify the weaknesses of "laser-painting" targets, together with the military advantage of pinpoint bombing accuracy. The result was a new breed of "smart bombs" that rely on the Global Positioning System, or GPS. The GPS is a satellite dependent system that constantly "maps" the planet, grid by grid. By programming the current crop of "smart bombs" with the target grid, bombs and cruise missiles can be guided by satellite to strike targets inside a three square yard radius hundreds of miles away! With a functioning GPS, these weapons are devastatingly accurate, while posing very little risk to the American military personnel that launch them. But without GPS guidance, they are as useless as an arsenal of bows and arrows.

On this date, the Global Positioning Satellite (GPS) technology will fail in receivers that are not upgraded or replaced. The GPS system consists of 24 satellites that transmit signals to earth, which are in turn picked up by electronic receivers to determine a vehicle's exact location and velocity. They are installed in both military and civilian vehicles and devices, including fighters, bombers, commercial and private airplanes, helicopters, trains, ships, submarines, tanks, jeeps, missiles and other "smart" weapons, police cars and ambulances, and some newer-model cars. Unfortunately, this system has a date-related error in its receiver technology. There are some 10 million of these receivers installed throughout the world. Those that are not upgraded will produce inaccurate data that could prove to be dangerous and even life threatening. While not specifically a Y2K-related problem, this computer glitch will add to the chaos and confusion.[39]

In addition to reducing America's arsenal to electronic junk, the GPS failure could cause widespread disruptions to civilian transportation and police services. Many large cities use GPS receivers to help guide emergency vehicles to their destinations. Some traffic, like trains and aircraft may have to be grounded until a reliable backup system of navigation is put on-line. The result could be sporadic shortages, food riots, and chaos in the larger cities.

But don't take our word for it; there are plenty of experts who have already identified areas of potential failure and assessed the possibility that the flaws can be corrected in time.

---

39 "Y2K: It's Closer Than You Think" by Michael S. Hyatt, *The Westergaard 2000 Group,* October 12, 1998.

About a year ago, I worked on an analysis
of the Global Positioning System (GPS)
ground station code to try to characterize
the Y2K problem. We found no less than 10
types of manifestations of the problem in a
survey of a randomly selected sample of 10
percent of the code. The occurrence of the
literal value "19" was only one of these 10
types. Other types included type overflow
problems at various dates throughout 1999,
Y2K arithmetic that implicitly assumed no
dates later than December 31, 1999, were
possible, and implicit module-interface
date-type conversions. These problems are
potentially infinite in their variety, and not
all can be detected with tools. Furthermore,
in GPS it is not possible to construct good
test cases to see what will happen at the
millennium start, because the future (time)
states of the system depend on physical values (orbital elements, pole wander, Jovian
gravitational force) that can be determined
with sufficient accuracy only from the
actual operation of the system within about
three months of the time of interest.
Approximately one percent of the total GPS
code is affected by this class of problems.

The GPS user-equipment code is in even deeper trouble because of the Y2K problem, and the breakage will occur well before January 1, 2000. Date, in the GPS signal standard, uses exactly 13 bits (these bits represent a time-unit offset from a conventional epoch date). This allocation is burned into proms on all existing GPS user equipment. On about August 20, 1999, the actual date value will overflow this 13-bit type, and the equipment will fail to produce correct time or position information. Best estimate is that there are 10^6 (10,000,000) pieces of user equipment that will be immediately affected. Everybody who depends indirectly on those pieces of equipment (meaning all the rest of us) will also be affected. The GPS standards committee is desperately trying to figure out what to do with the problem.

Various well-calibrated software estimation models (SLAM, REVIC, PRICE-S) predict that fixing the Y2K problem in systems of about 500,000 lines of code or larger will take more time than is available between now and the year 2000, regardless of how many programmers are thrown at the job.

Most of the US's military command-and-control systems contain more than 500,000 lines of code.

GPS is now the primary means of distributing time standards throughout the US and throughout much of the world. (The accuracy of the atomic clocks on board the GPS satellites is second only to those maintained by the primary standards clocks in Washington.) Thousands of large financial computers ultimately take their time calibration from GPS every day. Interest on overnight multi-billion-dollar short-term electronic-funds transactions is computed at millisecond granularity, derived from the GPS standard.[40]

09/09/99
+ + +

There are other possible problem dates. Since some programmers have used combinations of the number nine to tell a computer to reset, the first hurdle comes not on 01/01/00, but on 01/01/99, the first time two nines appear in the date field. The system will be challenged again on

40 Jack K. Horner, March 27, 1997, from an Internet Y2K forum entitled "Risks Associated with the Y2K Problem."

January 9, 1999, when there will be three nines in the date field and again on September 9, 1999, when all numbers are nines.

A common programming convention is to use a series of four nines in a row to designate the end of a file or the termination of a program. But what will happen on September 9, 1999, which a computer may read as 9999?

> Some of the computer's applications may not run at all, said Dave Wessels, an engineer with Cincinnati-based Tominy Inc., a computer company that provides Y2K services.

> "Others may run, but they may produce inaccurate results." he said. "That could be the worst problem."

> Even though the bug could be triggered by the date, the bug is a code problem, said Wayne Spalding, director of sales and marketing for EasiRun USA Inc., a Dayton-based provider of COBOL-based computer development tools and Y2K services.

> Fixing the bug, Spalding said, means not only changing the end-of-file marker but also ensuring the computer understands the new marker. "It's more of a logic error

and we have to make sure the logic is right before we convert data," Spalding said. The computer's logic error comes from the fact that the 9999 line, when used as an end-of-file marker, resembles a date but is not intended to be a date.

Chris Meyer, president of Sydney-based Sydney Microsystems, said the 9999 bug warrants immediate attention because its deadline is less than one year away.

The 9999 bug is just a piece of the whole computer date puzzle, which consists mainly of the Y2K problem, which stems from a computer's inability to process "00" as 2000 instead of 1900 on January 1, 2000. Fixes for the Y2K bug include programming the computer to understand "00" as 2000.[41]

Most of the software that operates main-frame computers like those that control the nation's infrastructure is custom written. Custom written software presents unique problems, since the code is written individually. Unless the original programmer is still available, any subsequent programmer

---

41 "Bugged by Another Date," *Dayton Business News,* September 28, 1998.

will have to first learn the programming "short-hand" that is as unique to individual program writers as a writing style is for book authors. A misinterpretation of a programmer's shorthand could introduce a whole new crop of programming bugs in addition to those related to the date.

In fact, it's only rollover errors that necessarily occur at the change of century and even those may not be detected until well after they (technically) occur. All other date-logic errors will occur either before or after that point in time (and may be detected at some other time). We all know that date-logic failures have been occurring for several years, with the earlier ones generally patched or temporarily worked around until more permanent solutions could be implemented.

So what we have is <u>a failure curve</u>. We know it started several years ago and we can fairly confidently predict that it will extend for some time into the new century. The open and very difficult question is: what is its shape? Despite the difficulty in answering that question, it's an important question to ask because if we can predict its shape accurately, then reports of early failures (when they materialize) would give us a reasonable basis for predicting not only the extent of the damage likely to occur but also when it is most likely to occur. There are a couple of riders to all the above points. First, the point at which date-logic becomes corrupt is not necessarily the date at which an externally discernible failure occurs; so what lead time to (evident) failure should we add? Second, any major failures may be difficult to hide but a single minor failure may prove merely inconvenient and be easily hidden. Multiple, successive, minor failures (quite a probable scenario for many organizations) may simply add inconvenience or could, by a process of attrition, *bring the organization to a grinding halt . . .* which should dispel the myth that "it all happens on January 1, 2000." It doesn't and it won't.[42]

In the real world, by the time Millennial Midnight has come and gone, there will be very, very few people who will *not* know far more than they wanted to about the Millennium Bug. The

---

42 "Predicting the Failure Curve," by Ian Hugo, *Westergaard Year 2000,* November 5, 1998.

pre-millennium bugs will provide plenty of advance warning of what is to come. Unfortunately, the warning will come much too late to do anything about it.

Chapter Six

WHISTLING
IN THE DARK

Gauging the Threat

+ + +

s we have already pointed out, there is no absolute way to predict just how bad the first months of the 21st century are going to be. We can only be sure that, come Millennial Midnight and beyond, you will be worse off, in some way, than you were prior to the "dawn of the new millennium." There are four distinct views regarding the severity of any coming computer disruptions, ranging from the "pie in the sky" view of BofA economist Wilson[43] to the most dire warnings of experts like Dr. Yardeni.[44]

The "Non-Event" Scenario

+ + +

The most comforting scenario is the hopeful fiction that we will fix the problem in plenty of time. Accepting this probability is the most palatable, and as a result, enjoys a surprisingly strong following among those who get all their information from the TV news. It's a pipe dream, but we'll explore the possibility nonetheless.

The Office of Management and Budget holds the responsibility for making sure the government will survive the century date change. On July 10, 1997, its director, Clinton appointee Sally Katzen,

---

43 See Chapter Four.
44 *ibid.*

gave her assessment of the government's readiness to Congress.

> "We have made a good start. While we, like the Subcommittees, are concerned about the limited time we have left, and the large amount of work that remains to be done, we are confident that we will finish that work so that the year 2000 computer problem will be a non-event—and we will all be able to celebrate the new millennium."[45]

Ms. Katzen is so far removed from reality that her comments defy explanation. In her view, we will solve the problem in time, under budget, and with a little time left over for a few rounds of golf before we shuffle off to watch the ball drop from Times Square at a giant, carefree New Year's Eve party. We'd like her to be correct. We really would.

Reality Check
+ + +

Unfortunately, she's not. Representative Steven Horn, Chairman of the House Subcommittee on Government Information, Management and

---

45 Sally Katzen, Director of Management and Budget: Before The Subcommittee on Technology of the Committee on Science and the Subcommittee on Government Management, Information, and Technology of the Committee on Government Reform and Oversight, US House of Representatives, July 10, 1997.

Technology, issued the following report to Congress on July 30, 1996, on the government's readiness for Y2K.

> "As Chairman of the Subcommittee on Government Management, Information and Technology, I am releasing the results of a survey sent to 24 major departments and agencies. The survey, which was sent on April 29, 1996, requested that agencies provide the subcommittee with a status report of when and at what expense agencies plan to address the problem of computer software which currently is unable to recognize the year 2000."

The following chart shows the exact state of the federal government's Y2K readiness. Despite Sally Katzen's assurances that Y2K will be a "non-event" scenario, in light of the facts, her assurances have a hollow ring.

It is significant to note that even the most rosy predictions, such as the National Science Institute's 100 percent compliance rating, is as of <u>March 1999</u>. Since it will take a *full year's* testing to ensure each calendar date change is bug-free, by definition, even those parts of the federal government that get the highest marks will, by definition, *already be too late*! Like it or not, January

Mission Critical Systems of Federal Departments and Agencies

Year 2000 Progress—As of September 1998

Agency	Year Complete	By 3/99	Feb 98	May 98	Aug 98
Social Security	1999	99%	A	A+	A
National Science Foundation	1999	100%	A	A-	A
Small Business Admin	1999	98%	B	B	A
General Services	1999	91%	C	A-	B+
Commerce	1999	100%	B	B	B
EPA	1999	92%	B	B	B
VA	1999	88%	A	C	B-
FEMA	1999	92%	C	A-	B-
NASA	2000	74%	D	B	C+
Agriculture	1999	89%	B	D	C
HUD	1999	78%	B	C	C
Treasury	2000	61%	D	C	D+
DOT	1999	70%	F	F	D
Office of Personnel Mngt.	2000	65%	B	C-	D
DOD	2001	54%	F	D	D
Labor	2001	52%	F	C	D
Interior	2005	37%	C-	C-	D
Nuclear Reg. Commission	2001	43%	C-	B	D
Health & Human Svces	2002	48%	D	F	F
Dept of Energy	2002	47%	D-	F	F
Dept. of State	2027	37%	F	F	F
Dept. of Justice	2030+	31%	C-	D	F
Dept of Education	2030+	29%	F	D	F
Agency for Int'l Devel	2023	16%	D-	F	D
Administration Overall		66%	D-	F	D

Source: Congressional Subcommittee on Government Management, Information and Technology

1, 1999, is <u>the</u> deadline. In his readiness report to the Congress, Rep. Horn also laid out, in bullet form, exactly as reproduced here, his committee's official assessment of government readiness. Not the "pie in the sky" assessment of a political appointee, but the cold, hard assessment of readiness as compiled by his sub-committee's auditors. Rep. Horn paints a very different picture from the one presented by Ms. Katzen. (The bracketed comments are those of the authors.)

> •"Major departments are in the initial planning stages of this effort, even though agencies need to have their systems inventoried and fixed by 1998 in order to provide sufficient time to test and ensure total accuracy. This means, *in the next year and a half these departments must complete their plans, inventory and fix million of lines of code, while simultaneously meeting agency needs.*" [Didn't make it—ed.]
> •"Even those agencies considered leaders on this issue, such as *the Social Security Administration and the Department of Defense,* <u>are not close</u> *to completing the inventory and solution stages of conversion.*" [SSA is closest, but close only counts in horseshoes and hand-grenades. They didn't make it, either.]

• "According to the information received, <u>only six agencies have cost estimates</u> on the monetary resources needed to solve the problem. In fact the Department of Health and Human Services has cost estimates for only two divisions, amounting to $125 million." [Estimated costs for repairs run into the *billions* of dollars.]

• "The Department of Agriculture has cost estimates for only one division, amounting to $5.6 million. The total estimate for these six agencies and their departments is $298 million."

• "The Department of Defense <u>has not yet completed its inventory of computer soft-ware code which needs to be converted</u>. The cost estimate to fix the 358 million estimated lines of code to be reviewed could cost $1.02 and $8.52 per line. This means the cost to review and fix DOD systems could range somewhere between $358 million and $3 billion." [Assuming they had time. The best estimates say the DOD won't even have its *mission critical* systems up and running for at least another decade.]

• "NASA, one of the most innovative, advanced and computer dependent agencies in the Federal government <u>has not</u>

<u>prepared a plan to solve the problem</u> and does not anticipate having a plan completed until March 1997—this leaves less than a year to inventory, and fix systems." [Not gonna make it, either.]

• "The Department of Transportation, which includes <u>the Federal Aviation Administration</u>, <u>Federal Highway Administration</u> and the <u>Federal Railroad Administration</u> *did not respond to the questions* as of this date." [Hard to fix what you haven't checked, but that's the government for you.]

• "The Department of Energy *did not begin to address the year 2000 issue* <u>until a week after</u> <u>it received subcommittee's survey.</u>"[46] [The Department of Energy, in addition to making sure the lights come on, is also in charge of our nuclear weapons manufacturing and readiness program. They'll get to Y2K eventually. We hope.]

It is significant to note that Ms. Katzen's "don't worry, be happy" scenario to Congress was issued one full year *after* Representative Horn's report.

---

46 Statement of the Honorable Stephen Horn, Chairman Subcommittee on Government Management, Information and Technology to the 104th Congress, July 30, 1996.

Although Katzen's report to Congress in July 1997 was upbeat and filled with assurances, she is directly contradicted by a report issued by her own agency, the Office of Management and Budget, which she presumably read only a few months before. That report neglected to mention Y2K as a "non-event"; in fact, the OMB report says quite the opposite.

"With the arrival of the year 2000, people will know that the year '00' stands for 2000. However, the hardware and software in many computer systems will not understand this new meaning. Unless they are fixed or replaced, they <u>will</u> fail at the turn of the century in one of three ways:

1. they will reject legitimate entries, or

2. they will compute erroneous results, or

3. they <u>will simply not run</u>.

"Many systems which compare dates to decide which is earlier will <u>no longer work</u>. Comparisons of dates permeate Federal computer systems—they are how inventories are maintained (e.g., last in, first out), how the order of filings is handled (e.g., first come, first served), and how eligibility is determined (e.g., an applicant must have filed before a certain date).

"Systems which calculate length of time also may not compute accurately. Computations of length of time are common in Federal computer systems—they are how benefits are computed (e.g., based on length of time), how eligibility is determined (e.g., based on length of service), and how expiration dates are calculated (e.g., expires after three years).

"There are other possible effects of the date change in computer software, depending on the assumptions made and programming technique used by the designer of the software. For example, information relevant to a year could be found by using the year to find the information in a table. For example, information about 1997 would be at the 97th location in the table. Such a technique would fail in the year '00' because there is no 0th location."[47]

The "non-event" scenario, sadly, is actually a "non-scenario" event. The overwhelming body of evidence points in a different direction, so we'll waste no more time on the Sally Katzens of this world. Instead, we'll examine what are the most

---

47 Report of the US Office of Management and Budget, February 6, 1997.

likely of the *realistic* probabilities facing us in a few short months.

The Temporary Inconvenience Scenario
✦ ✦ ✦

This is the scenario alluded to by BofA chief economist John Wilson in Chapter Four. In his view, "We'll all stock up for five to seven days worth of food, water, clothing and cash."

To a large extent, this is the scenario that we adopted for Ryan Tyler and his family. Within a week, in our story, limited energy and telecommunications services had been restored. But, as Tyler found out, a week without food, water, clothing and cash is an eternity! By the end of that week, his entire world had collapsed as effectively as if it were a post nuclear war zone.

If the power goes down for a week, then repairs to the infrastructure can't even *begin* until power is restored. Computers run on electricity. You can't fix 'em if you can't boot 'em! And nothing can come back on line until after they are fixed. That's a Catch-22 situation that the minimalists seem to have factored out in their assessment.

Obviously, the "temporary inconvenience" scenario only works if you have also taken temporary leave of your senses.

The Partial
Disruption Scenario
✦ ✦ ✦

There are those who envision a kind of "partial disruption," but on a more or less long-term basis. This view makes the assumption that 90 to 95 percent of the defective embedded chips will be replaced and noncompliant computer code will have been re-written in time. In this scenario, damage is limited to state and local computer systems and medium to small business networks. Thanks to the cascade effect, these failures will have serious implications, but by and large will be isolated failures rather than a global blackout.

Michael S. Hyatt is the author of *"The Millennium Bug,"*[48] subtitled "How to Survive the Coming Chaos." In his book, he develops three possible scenarios that he calls brownout, blackout and meltdown. The Partial Disruption Scenario corresponds to Hyatt's view of the brownout, but he takes it much further.

Brownout
✦ ✦ ✦

Hyatt's scenario begins with intermittent power disruptions and power "brownouts" that bring

---

48 *The Millennium Bug* by Michael S. Hyatt is published by Regnery Publishing Inc., Washington, DC.

business and industry to its knees. In the brownout scenario, water treatment plants and water delivery systems will break down as the embedded chips that regulate them begin to suffer the effects of Y2K. Air traffic control computers fail, grounding commercial aircraft. Rail traffic will grind to a halt as computers lose track of trains, misdirect traffic, or simply go black altogether. Goods grow scarce as the transportation infrastructure breaks down, and prices begin to rise. If the telephones work at all, they will be jammed by callers struggling to report outages or report other problems. Banks will begin to generate ridiculous errors, clogging the system with even more calls. ATM's will fail or will report incorrect balances. International wire transfers and other Electronic Funds Transfers will be affected. Some government agencies will simply cease to exist. The IRS will be so hopelessly lost following the collapse of its computer system that Congress will be forced to enact a flat tax to keep the government funded. The military, while functioning, will suffer crippling damage to its electronic warfare capabilities. The extent of that damage will become a military secret. Police services, while functioning, will be seriously impacted. Some police departments will lose their communications systems entirely. The Canadian federal government is concerned

enough about the potential for anarchy that it is
making contingency plans for just such an emergency. Soldiers and federal police, like the Royal
Canadian Mounted Police, have been told not to
make any plans between the end of December and
the middle of March—just in case.

> Every Canadian soldier's leave may be can-
> celled to keep the full force ready in case
> the Millennium Bug begins wreaking
> havoc at 12:01 AM, January 1, 2000. The
> military's plans come as the RCMP imposes
> a no-holiday rule on its members across
> Canada between December 27, 1999, and
> March 15, 2000. "There is consideration
> being given to that because we would be
> heavily tasked . . . to wait until the stroke of
> midnight to see what happens," Capt. Mike
> Audette, public affairs officer for Land Force
> Western Area, said. He said the Canadian
> Forces could impose a blanket leave-cancel-
> lation from December 1999 through March
> 2000 or implement some type of recall
> mechanism to have a certain number of per-
> sonnel on standby in case of problems.[49]

Hospitals will lose critical computerized systems that may cause life support systems to shut

49 *Edmonton* [Alberta] *News,* October 23, 1998.

down. The Food and Drug Administration issued a friendly reminder to medical appliance manufacturers, including the manufacturers of appliances like pacemakers.

> This is to remind you that some computer systems and software applications currently used in medical devices, including embedded microprocessors, may experience problems beginning January 1, 2000, due to their use of two-digit fields for date representation. In addition to adversely affecting the functioning of some devices, the two-digit date format could also affect computer-controlled design, production or quality control processes.[50]

The letter, dated June 25, 1997, and signed by Bruce Burlington, M.D. Director, Center for Devices and Radiological Health, *suggested* that manufacturers "conduct hazard and safety analyses to determine whether device performance could be affected by the year-2000 date change." Dr. Burlington's letter also suggested, "If these analyses show that device safety or effectiveness could be affected, then appropriate steps *should* be taken to correct current production and to

---

50 Bruce Burlington, M.D., Director, Center for Devices and Radiological Health.

assist customers who have purchased such devices."[51]

All of us should be inspired with confidence, knowing that the manufacturers of medical appliances were the recipients of a letter suggesting that they place patients before profits and spend millions on a problem that doesn't yet exist, in real time! Remember, the federal government knew about the problem more than a *decade* ago. If medical manufacturers didn't care then, why should they care now? Especially since the only federal directives are *suggestions*, not FDA directives. If FDA suggestions really had an effect on industry, tobacco products would be illegal. Money talks, so people die to ensure future profits for the tobacco industry. The medical appliance manufacturing industry has lobby money, too. So don't expect to see the federal government forcing compliance until *after* people begin to keel over. By then, it will be too late. Patients with pacemakers should contact their doctor to see if Y2K poses any risk to their appliance's ability to operate after 01/01/00.

Y2K could make hospitals among the most dangerous places to be at the turn of the century.

---

51 Bruce Burlington, M.D., Director, Center for Devices and Radiological Health.

Patients dependent on electronic life support systems and other life saving devices are at the greatest risk. Millennial Midnight could set modern medicine back to where it was during World War I.

> "As an example of how a noncompliant microcontroller might seriously cause an item of non-computer equipment to malfunction, consider an item of medical equipment in a hospital emergency room which measures the flow of blood or plasma into a patient. The microcontroller in this hypothetical medical equipment keeps track of when the equipment was last calibrated and automatically shuts the equipment down as unsafe if it is not calibrated on schedule. If the microcontroller is not Year 2000 compliant, on January 1, 2000, it might compare '00' to the date of last calibration (say, June 1, 1999, or '99') and miscalculate that 99 years had passed since the last calibration, shutting down the equipment."[52]

---

52 Congressional Oversight Hearing on Financial Institutions and the Year 2000 Problem Prepared Testimony of Jeff Jinnett, President, LeBoeuf Computing Technologies, Thursday, July 10, 1997.

Billing problems could bankrupt the health care industry entirely. Food riots will be possible in some places as shortages get worse, and the economy will be plunged into a recession. In Hyatt's view, brownout is the <u>best case</u> scenario.

The Case for the Brownout Scenario

+ + +

The brownout sounds pretty grim, but it has a far greater base of support among IT experts than the "non-event" scenario presented by Sally Katzen. On the other hand, Hyatt's frightening picture of a post Y2K brownout has plenty of evidence to support it.

Quintus Corporation, a provider of software and services that turn contacts into loyal customers, today announced the results of a survey, revealing that the majority of call centers are not ready for the glut of consumer calls about the Year 2000 (Y2K) issue. The survey, conducted at Quintus' Consultant Pavilion at the Computer Telephony Demo and Expo in late September, was compiled from the written responses of approximately 150 call center executives and technicians. Call centers—simply put, the toll-free numbers that customers call with orders, inquiries or complaints—are for many companies the only point of direct contact with consumers. As Y2K problems continue to grow, increasing numbers of consumers will phone these centers with questions and concerns. As Quintus' survey revealed, few companies have the ability to deal with the anticipated increase in calls. Among the more alarming statistics: only 29 percent of companies surveyed have a Y2K task force to assess call center issues and concerns. Fewer than half surveyed—only 42 percent—reported that their companies are prepared to handle the volume of calls from consumers concerned about the Year 2000 issue.[53]

Even if the telephone system does survive Y2K, and that is a big "if" at this point, lines will be so snarled with callers that most traffic won't get through. That includes calls to 911 or to doctors or hospitals, electronic funds transfers (which are transmitted over telephone lines), internet connections, ATM machines, check verification systems, and so on.

---

53 *Business Wire*, October 13, 1998.

The economic impact of Y2K on the domestic economy will be severe, even if the critical infrastructure is only interrupted for a matter of days or weeks. Y2K expert Dr. Ed Yardeni is on record as saying the United States faces a 60 percent chance of a "nasty" recession in 1999, even before Y2K completely rears its ugly head. We'll discuss the economic impact of Y2K in each of these scenarios in Chapter Seven.

The Blackout Scenario
+ + +

A total "blackout"—the loss of a substantial portion, or even all of the nation's power grid, is a far more terrifying scenario than most of us give any thought to. We can picture the "temporary interruption" scenario; most of us have experienced that to some degree, at some point in our lives. We can even picture the "brownout scenario," although it's a little fuzzier picture. During the energy crisis in the '70s, power brownouts were not uncommon. But those "brownouts" were controlled events designed to conserve energy. As such, they were planned to cause minimum disruption. And society was nowhere near as computer dependent as it is today. So, although we can picture a kind of modified brownout scenario, a total blackout of uncertain duration is completely foreign to the experience of most Americans.

The Great Depression Revisited

✦ ✦ ✦

A Y2K blackout will result in bank runs on a scale unseen since the days following the Crash of 1929. In the blackout scenario, the only way to get access to your money will be in person at the old fashioned teller window. As we've already pointed out, there isn't nearly enough cash on hand to meet the demands of depositors. We can count on the government to order the banking system to shut down for a "cooling off" period, much as they did back in the '30s. And like the '30s, many of the banks that do close their doors will never reopen them again.

The Emergency Powers Act authorizes the President to invoke martial law. The Emergency Powers Act was written expressly for this kind of scenario. All infrastructure issues will be turned over to the Federal Emergency Management Administration (FEMA) for the duration.

During a period of martial law, FEMA's control over the civilian infrastructure is total. The Constitution is suspended, and the United States of America becomes a police state. The Congressional Record reflects the debate that ensued in 1933, when the Congress passed the Farm Bill to meet the challenges to social order

presented by the Great Depression. Congressman
Beck saw such a move in the context of his day.

> "I think of all the damnable heresies that
> have ever been suggested in connection
> with the Constitution, the doctrine of
> emergency is the worst. It means that when
> Congress declares an emergency, there is
> no Constitution. This means its death. It is
> the very doctrine that the German chan-
> cellor is invoking today in the dying hours
> of the parliamentary body of the German
> republic, namely, that because of an emer-
> gency, it should grant to the German chan-
> cellor absolute power to pass any law, even
> though the law contradicts the Constitu-
> tion of the German republic. Chancellor
> Hitler is at least frank about it. We pay the
> Constitution lipservice, but the result is
> the same."

The Farm Bill of 1933
+ + +

In 1933, the House passed the Farm Bill by a vote
of more than three to one. The Farm Bill was an
emergency measure that gave the US government
sweeping powers over agriculture. And, according to the US Senate, the emergency was never
lifted. Senate Report 93-549, issued in 1973,

says, "Since March the 9th, 1933, the United States has been in a state of declared national emergency." Congressman Beck's Congressional Record tells us:

> "This vast range of powers, taken together, confer enough authority to rule the country without reference to normal constitutional processes. Under the powers delegated by these statutes, the President may: seize property; organize and control the means of production; seize commodities; assign military forces abroad; institute martial law; seize and control all transportation and communication; regulate the operation of private enterprise; restrict travel; and, in a plethora of particular ways, control the lives of all American citizens."

Those who think that the declaration of martial law is unlikely, even in a blackout scenario, think again! The declaration has already been made and never lifted. The Constitutional separation of powers between the three branches of government, the executive, the legislative and the courts has *already* been *legally* dissolved. The only thing barring the implementation of the provisions of martial law is a reason. Y2K will supply that.

You Can't Eat Money

+ + +

Executive Order 10998 was signed by John F. Kennedy in 1962. It provides for government control over foods and food production.

National Guard and federal troops will be mobilized to handle the distribution of food, water, and emergency supplies. Until the stockpiles run out, as they will do early on. It takes a lot of food and water to feed 250 million people. Since a blackout will disrupt and even paralyze the distribution network, many areas will run out of emergency supplies very early in the crisis. Rationing of food and fresh water will result in chaos. The probability of food riots, even in small to mid-sized cities, is high. The government will have the authority to enact curfews, and troops will be authorized to use deadly force to maintain order, no questions asked.

A blackout will eliminate the government's ability to raise money. The IRS will cease to exist. Congress can enact a flat tax, but very little of a post blackout economy will involve cash. We see an example of that today in post-Soviet Russia. One estimate says that 87 percent of Russia's domestic economy is now based on the barter system. It is going to be difficult for the government to collect a value-added tax when the currency involved is a box of ammunition being exchanged for a chicken. Does the government take a third of the bullets or a third of the chicken? The Russians found a solution to that problem by borrowing its operating capital from the West, primarily from America. Despite massive infusions of Western aid, Russia's government still teeters, at the time of this writing, on the verge of collapse.

A Y2K blackout will be global in scope, hitting the world's leading industrialized nations more or less uniformly. Where will Washington go to borrow money? Even if we could, you can't eat money, as the Russians have already discovered.

Moscow's inability to pay its troops has resulted in a demoralized military in which the only trend more prevalent than suicide among troops of all ranks is the rate of desertion. American troops are unlikely to put themselves at risk of life and limb, particularly at the hands of their countrymen, before many of them decide to just go home and defend their own families and property.

Don't Get Sick

+ + +

One of the least desirable places to find oneself in the event of a Y2K blackout will be the nation's hospitals. Without electricity, critical life support equipment will fail. Operations will be performed without modern sanitation, in poor lighting, and with none of the electrical appliances, like suction machines, electric bone saws, patient monitoring devices, and so on.

According to the definition in the Federal Food, Drug, and Cosmetic (FD&C) Act, a "device" is: "An instrument, apparatus, implement, machine, contrivance, implant, in vitro reagent, or other similar or related article, including any component, part or accessory, which is intended for use in the diagnosis of disease or other conditions, or in the cure, mitigation, treatment, or prevention of disease, in man or other animals, or intended to affect the structure or any function of the body and which does not achieve its primary intended purposes through chemical action and which is not dependent upon being metabolized for the achievement of its primary intended purposes." As this definition suggests, many different types of products are properly regulated as medical devices. *Medical devices include over 100,000 products in more than 1,700 categories.* The products regulated by FDA as medical devices range from

simple everyday articles, such as ther-
mometers, tongue depressors, and heating
pads, to the more complex devices, such
as pacemakers, intrauterine devices, and
kidney dialysis machines.[54]

In a very real sense, medicine in the early part
of the 21st century will more closely resemble
health care as it was in the early days of the 20th
century. Think of it! Most of the medical advances
of the past 100 years will simply vanish when the
lights go off. Emergency medical technicians will
have to make do without such advancements as
remote defibrillators, real time communication
with hospital emergency rooms and doctors, radio
communications between ambulances and dis-
patchers, and, in some cases, without ambulances
at all!

Forget about life-saving devices like the "Jaws
of Life" used to extricate victims from car wrecks,
or rapid response teams for major medical emergencies like train wrecks, natural gas explosions,
or nuclear disasters at the nation's nuclear power
plants. Even some implanted medical devices
like pacemakers may not function properly.

54 Statement By Michael A. Friedman, M.D., Acting
Commissioner, FDA, to The Special Committee on the Year
2000 Technology Problem, July 23, 1998.

Devices include: conversion of pacemaker telemetry data; conversion, transmission, or storage of medical images; off-line analysis of ECG data; digital analysis and graphical presentation of ECG data; *calculation of rate response for a cardiac pacemaker*; perfusion calculations for cardiopulmonary bypass; and calculation of bone fracture risk from bone densitometry data. Since there is a chance that the two-digit format may affect the performance of these software devices, we believe that the Year 2000 risk needs to be mitigated through proactively working with manufacturers.[55]

Meltdown

+ + +

Of all the possible Y2K scenarios, the meltdown scenario is the most frightening. In a meltdown scenario, banks won't close temporarily; they will shut down altogether. Currency will cease to exist as money. In post World War I Germany, the defeated forces of Kaiser Wilhelm returned home to find their economy in shambles. The accumulated savings of a lifetime simply vanished as

---

55 Statement By Michael A. Friedman, M.D., Acting Commissioner, FDA, to The Special Committee on the Year 2000 Technology Problem, July 23, 1998.

hyper inflation eroded the value of currency to the degree that it became more valuable as kindling for wood stoves than it was as money. At the last the German government was issuing currency denoted in billions of marks, and it took a wheelbarrow full of them to purchase a loaf of bread.

In the event of meltdown, the only money that will have any value at all is "hard money"—gold and silver coins, and other precious metals whose value is directly commensurate with how badly the seller wants to accept it in exchange for his wares.

Currency is not the same as money, although we have come to think of it as such in our society. In reality, money is a different animal altogether. Simply stated, money is an instrument of value that can be exchanged for goods and services. It retains its value only as long as people are confident that it will continue to be accepted as an instrument of trade.

For example, would you consider selling your brand-new car for 2000 American greenbacks? Of course not. But if you lived in 1920, it would be a very good deal, indeed. You could take your $2000, replace the car with a better one, and still have a four-figure bank account. In 1920, a new Ford could be had for less than $750. Today, a new Ford is worth 20,000 or more American greenbacks. The $19,250 difference is the result

of 70 years of inflation. Granted, a modern automobile has more whistles and bells than a 1920
Model T, but relatively speaking, a car is a car,
and the Model T was as good as Detroit could
offer at the time.

The reason that a new car costs so much more
now is because people won't accept anything less
to sell one to you. Currency is not money—it is
an expression of trust. Once people don't trust its
buying power, it becomes worthless.

No Government to Help
+ + +

In the blackout scenario, the government is ham-
strung by the collapse of the national infrastructure. It will be unable to raise operating capital
until after the crisis has passed. In the meantime,
it will continue to function in some limited fashion, mainly on the hope that the crisis will pass.
Hope then becomes the currency by which the
government continues to fund limited operations.
Hope that Washington will one day honor its
IOU's to its employees and military forces; hope
that one day America will resume its place as the
global leader, hope that one day all this will be
behind us. People have an amazing capacity to
survive on hope alone, provided that hope is realistic enough to sustain them.

In a total meltdown, that hope is gone. The federal government will survive only as long as it can maintain the fiction that Millennial Midnight is temporary. A total meltdown of our infrastructure will expose the emperor's new clothes for what they are.

In a blackout scenario, we can expect to see widespread hunger when the transportation grid fails temporarily. Food will be rationed, but there will be enough to maintain survival in the short term. In a meltdown, the operative word would be starvation. The transportation grid remains down until local food supplies are exhausted, and there is no way to replenish the existing stocks. America has a grain reserve at the time of this writing sufficient for some 40 days or so. With rationing, it might be extended for as long as 90 days. But that assumes that there is still a government to oversee the rationing program 90 days after America becomes a technological wasteland.

In the event of meltdown, the food reserves will be long gone before alternative food supplies can be developed. There are a relative handful of food producers in America, and food production over the last 20 years or so has become more or less completely dependent on modern computer-operated machinery and similar technology.

Without that modern technology, farmers and

other food producers will be forced to revert to long-forgotten farming techniques as high tech as those employed by a modern city dweller's back yard vegetable garden. Without irrigation, of course. In a meltdown, water treatment plants and pumping stations will be a distant memory.

We live in a wired world. Computers do so much of the work for us that we have forgotten how to get the same results manually. Today's food producers learn how to operate the machines that do the work, not how to do the work itself. Farmers will be as prepared to harvest crops as city dwellers will be to hunt, kill, and dress a deer.

So, Which Is It?
+ + +

So, what's it going to be? Will it be a non-event, a brownout, blackout, or meltdown? Nobody can say for certain. The best we can do is to rely on the educated guesses of those in the Information Technology industry.

Michael Hyatt cites an informal survey conducted on the Internet among IT professionals in his book *The Millennium Bug*. A computer programmer named Phil Edwards surveyed an international group of 38 computer experts and Y2K researchers. He asked them to grade the probabilities, using the following scale.

5=probable collapse of the economy and a shutdown of our national infrastructure, economic depression, martial law and a breakdown of the health care system. (The Blackout Scenario)

3=the demise of noncompliant government agencies, banking problems, a temporary interruption in the power grid and transportation system and an economic recession. (Brownout Scenario)

1=Non-event Event—Millennium Midnight comes and goes and everybody has a Happy New Year.

According to Hyatt:

Voting on a scale of 1 to 5, experts used the Delphi Technique and the Internet to state their opinion on the issue. The 38 respondents had a total of 669 years of experience, or an average of 17.6 years each. The average score was 3.96.[56]

The conclusion of the experts is that Y2K will plunge America into a scenario hovering somewhere between blackout and brownout. To put it

56 *The Millennium Bug*, Michael S. Hyatt, Regnery Press, page 180.

another way, 21st century America could find itself in a technological time warp that will hover somewhere between 1850 and 1950. Anybody remember how to shoe a horse?

Chapter Seven

Y2K AND THE GLOBAL ECONOMY

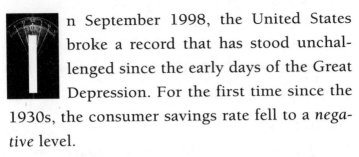n September 1998, the United States broke a record that has stood unchallenged since the early days of the Great Depression. For the first time since the 1930s, the consumer savings rate fell to a *negative* level.

The savings rate—the portion of after-tax dollars left over after spending—fell to –0.2 percent, the first negative monthly savings rate since the department began reporting the figures on a monthly basis in 1959. Prior to that, figures were calculated quarterly. The last time there was a negative savings rate was in 1933, when the rate was -2.1 percent, a department official said. The savings rate has been falling steadily for years, but a change by the Commerce Department in July in how it calculates the rate has made it appear even smaller. The new method defines consumers' after-tax income more narrowly and now excludes certain types of mutual-fund distributions that made income appear stronger under the old measure. The gain in spending in September matched forecasts by US economists in a Reuters survey, though the income gain exceeded the 0.1 percent rise that was projected. Analysts have been impressed by consumers' willingness to spend despite financial turmoil in the United States and around the world that has dented confidence in the economy's health.[57]

The decline in savings is part of a disturbing economic trend that began in the early 1990s, as the bull market settled in for the long term. For most of the decade, consumer debt has remained at an all time high, while personal savings steadily declined to its current levels. At the same time, personal bankruptcy levels are rising exponentially.

Easy Come, Easy Go

+ + +

One reason that consumers are saving so little is because the lure of easy money on the stock market is so profound. With interest rates hovering below six percent, and the market offering an average annual return of 20 percent or more, the temptation to gamble with borrowed money is high. Some credit cards offer interest free loans of up to $10,000 for as long as 60 days, provided the principal is fully repaid before the grace period expires. In theory, a person can speculate for two months, repay the full amount, borrow it

---

57 *US Savings Rate Hits Lowest Level Since 1930s*, Reuters, October 31, 1998.

again, reinvest it for another two months, and so
on, picking up a tidy profit along the way. As
long as the market continues to perform, this
kind of strategy pays off big returns. Unless and
until the market goes south, that is.

> The consequences of failure are frighten-
> ing. Not only internal bank dealing and
> back-office systems, but interbank sys-
> tems, billing and payment systems, and
> the Fed's own FedWire interbank network
> could all fail. There is, *according to senior
> Wall Street analysts, a good chance of being
> plunged into recession.* The <u>Fed became
> seriously concerned</u> last year and began
> beating banks over the head to reach
> speedy solutions. The result is that New
> York is probably ahead of the rest of the
> world in fixing the bug. For what it is
> worth, the Central Intelligence Agency
> believes Britain, Canada and Australia are
> the next best prepared. But it still isn't
> clear whether <u>anyone</u> has done enough.[58]

Publicly, the Federal Reserve has maintained a
cautious public position on the financial community's Y2K readiness status. A recent four-day live

---

58 *Business Day (UK)*, November 13, 1998.

test involving the Security Industry Association was hailed as a "success," but officials are careful about declaring either victory or defeat.

The last thing they want is a loss of confidence and a run on deposits as the millennium approaches. And it defies belief that there will be no problems. So far it looks as though the Fed may have beaten Wall Street into shape to avoid its worst nightmare—a systemic collapse. To expect perfection, however, is probably wildly unrealistic.[59]

Get Out of Debt—Now!
+ + +

When the market does take a dive, those investors who have "mortgaged the farm" find themselves with huge credit card debt, no savings to cover the shortfall, and, for many, no way out short of filing for bankruptcy protection. This is one reason why the personal bankruptcy rate jumped nearly 300 percent in the first half of the 1990s. Personal bankruptcy has cost the economy so much already that Congress has passed laws tightening the rules for bankruptcy declaration in an effort reverse the trend.

---

59 *Business Day (UK)*, November 13, 1998.

This kind of "leveraging" helps maintain the fiction that fuels the global economy. That fiction is that the ledger sheet for the global economy is an expression of *wealth*, rather than what it truly is, which is an expression of *debt*. Every dollar in the current economic system is a *phantom* dollar. Ten thousand dollars of credit card debt, invested for 60 days might return 10 percent, or a "profit" of $1000. Except the $10,000 never really existed, except as an entry on a ledger book.

Thanks to computers, the global economy is a 24 hour a day operation, with money moving around the globe from one time zone to another. As long as it remains in motion, John Q. Investor's borrowed $10,000 remains an asset. When it grinds to a halt as the result of a market crash, it is exposed for what it really is—a $10,000 liability.

The Emperor Has No Clothes

✦ ✦ ✦

During the 1980s, it looked like the US was destined to become a subsidiary holding of the Bank of Japan. Japanese money fueled wild real estate speculation in Hawaii, Los Angeles, and New York. The "Asian Flu" slowed the movement of Japanese money sufficiently to expose the true nature of the "Asian miracle" as a speculative bubble. When it burst, those investors that tied their fortunes to the Japanese yen saw the value of their investments shrink as exponentially as they rose.

It's like the story about the Emperor's New Clothes. Everyone pretended that the Emperor's new suit of invisible clothes were just beautiful until an unsophisticated child pointed out the obvious. He didn't understand that it was politically correct to pretend and thereby not "rock the boat," and shouted: "The Emperor has no clothes on!" The rest of the population, relieved to find that they were not the only ones who doubted their own senses took up the cry, the emperor was exposed as a fool, and the empire collapsed.

As Japan's fortunes rose to unsustainable levels, investors began to recognize, one by one, that the Japanese miracle was without substance. As they pulled their investments and moved them to safer havens, the Japanese economy slowed. More investors recognized that the Asian "miracle" was based on illusion, and the economy went into recession. At the time of this writing, Japan is teetering on the brink of outright depression.

The irony is in the fact that Japan is the world's largest *creditor* economy. America, on the other hand, is the world's largest *debtor* economy. Many people think that the world owes America money.

Actually, it's the other way around. Japan is the third largest holder of American debt instruments. On the books, Japan is far more solvent than America. The *illusion* of wealth, maintained by the rapid movement of money from one market to the other, is the foundation upon which America's bull market miracle is built. Once that illusion is shattered, the global economy will collapse under the weight of its own debt.

Too Little, Too Late
+ + +

Japan's Prime Minister Hashimoto promised to cut taxes across the board in an effort to buoy up the struggling Japanese economy. The tax cuts were designed to persuade Japanese consumers to begin spending again. Japan has the world's second largest economy.

Hashimoto's austerity plan was designed to save the economy, but instead, it is plunging it closer to the abyss. The Japanese consumer is translating government austerity into personal austerity and has begun putting money away against a rainy day. If nobody is buying, then nobody is selling.

Japan's troubles intensified the economic problems already ongoing in much of the region. Some US analysts fear the effect could cross over

and even begin to damage the buoyant American
bull market as well. Will it?

The US trade deficit with Japan acts as a kind
of "safety valve," keeping the American economy
from overheating too quickly. But cheap imports
from Japan could well prompt America to impose
trade barriers. That could do us some damage. It
could trigger a global recession, although not the
worldwide depression that Sony Chairman Noria
Ogha is predicting. But it could well be the first
domino to fall in that direction, if Y2K plays out
the way many experts are predicting.

The US stock market, on the other hand, is
extremely vulnerable to a drop in share prices. The
market is dangerously overvalued, yet prices continue to climb. Almost twice as many Americans
hold shares in the market today as they did a
decade ago. A similar scenario played out in Japan
in the early '90s. Banks began to go bust, property
values began to drop, and market prices began to
slide. As a result, Japanese economic growth began
to slide to its current level of only 1.3 percent. In
the curious world of economics, that actually rep-
resents a net loss of 6 percent in economic output
over the last six years.

In a best case scenario, Japan's problems will
not affect the US economy all that severely. Most
of the damage fell on the shoulders of the Asian

economies around Japan. Japan only accounts for between one to two percent of the US GDP. Europe's investment in Japan is similarly small. But Japan's miracle economy of the '80s quickly became the global economic basket case of the '90s, conventional wisdom notwithstanding. American investors should be wary of further Asian market problems. Especially in light of the impending Y2K iceberg.

A Bug in the Hedges

+ + +

Much of the investment in Japan is highly leveraged and extremely vulnerable. One of the hottest vehicles for making money from Japan's economic misfortune is the "hedge fund." Basically, a hedge fund is really little more than a "bookie's bet" on what direction a nation's currency will go. We call it a "bookie's bet" because it works on a similar principle.

Fund managers spot an advantage and leverage it up by virtue of the size of the pool of investment money they control. Some currency plays have been "leveraged" up to 20 times; some went even higher.

Here's how it works. A leveraged turn of 3 percent leveraged up 20 times, gives a 60 percent return on your investment. This kind of investing is a sort of modified margin that pays very, very well, as long as the bet is right.

On the other hand, the "margin call" for this kind of investment is brutal. For example, in October 1998, forced closures of yen borrowing to buy US bonds posted losses of 20 percent or more. Using the same equation—that is, leveraged 20 times—means the same 3 percent investment, down 20 percent, would leverage <u>down</u> to a <u>loss</u> of *400 percent!*

Hedge funds speculate in currency and government bond fluctuations. Over the course of a day, these rates rise and fall many times. A difference of a few minutes can mean the difference of several percentage points in either direction. Most of this trading is calculated using sophisticated computer programs—*date dependent programs*—to work out potential profit and loss points, second by second throughout the business day. A date anomaly of a few seconds could mean billions of dollars in profits or losses.

The October 1998 hedge fund debacle was responsible for huge losses that resulted in a discernible credit crunch. It has already created a good deal of uncertainty throughout the global system. That uncertainty is already deepening the Japanese recession and postponing recovery. It will continue, even without Y2K, to have a deflationary effect on the global economy well into 2000.

As we pointed out earlier, Japan begins its fiscal year April 1, 1999. The Millennium Bug may bite early as a result, further eroding investor confidence. Just the threat of what Y2K might do could be enough to start the dominoes toppling, even before the calendar rolls over to any of the Y2K danger dates.

The Corporate Y2K Report Card

+ + +

The success of the global economy is largely due to a delicate balancing act where each component works in harmony with the other sectors of the business world. In order for continued success, each element is dependent upon the other. The global economy is *not* just the blue chip companies, but the small to medium size enterprises (SME's) that support them. For example, a major corporation like General Motors may be Y2K compliant. But if the factory that manufactures GM's seats can't fill GM's orders because their own computer system failed, GM's production grinds to a halt as effectively as if GM had not bothered to upgrade at all. We tend to think of Y2K in terms of how it will affect America. Thinking in those terms, if all of America's computer systems are Y2K compliant, then the problem goes away. Unfortunately, due to the very nature of the *global* economy, what affects one segment affects all, in America, or on the other side of the ocean. Consider the following article from the *London Sunday Times*.

> Last month, Action 2000 warned that SME's in particular were guilty of failing to act. "I am less optimistic about the fate of smaller companies in Britain than I was," says Don Cruickshank, chairman of Action 2000. Only 60 percent have assessed the risks of the bug to their business. "This makes for depressing reading for this crucial section of the economy," he says. . . . Most SME's do not even understand the scope of the problem. "Many businesses think it is just to do with PC's," says Gerard Long, senior manager for the year 2000 programme at Midland Bank. "They haven't understood the issues of embedded systems, supply chains or infrastructure risks, such as power failures. They haven't thought about contingency plans and they are *very vulnerable to glitches that could put them out of business*."
>
> No business is too remote to be affected— even if it does not have a computer.

Farmers, for example, could suffer equipment failures in their milking parlors or grain silos. Their feedstuff supplier could fail to deliver or the vet could lose all his records. The most unlikely equipment may be affected. It may not even be possible to drown your sorrows or toast the new millennium, as some pubs are finding that their beer pumps will not work after 1999.[60]

Horror stories abound. Not just the big ones, such as planes plummeting and guided missiles launching themselves, but much closer to home for the average SME: systems installed this year that are still not compliant; small software houses that may voluntarily liquidate rather than face the barrage of support queries; snake-oil solutions and bogus consultants who do more harm than good.

Company directors could be held legally responsible for the consequences of the bug, since it is regarded as a foreseeable risk. For the same reason, insurance companies may not cover millennium-related claims. . . . Ironically, one of the most

---

60 *The London Sunday Times*, November 1, 1998.

damaging effects of the bug may have been to make SME's too wary of new technology. "A big negative side is that it has stopped a lot of small businesses from buying a computer to make things easier for themselves," says Brendan Burns, vice-chairman of the Federation of Small Businesses.

What Do the Experts Say?

+ + +

Back in 1973, Americans kept over 10 times more money in the bank than they had in mutual funds. Even in 1990 Americans had three times more in the bank. But as of last year, the lines crossed: Now, America has more of its money in mutual funds than it does in banks. Millions of naive investors have been pouring their life savings into the market at an alarming rate. Since 1994, more than 30 million new investors have bellied up to the trough, hoping to cash in on market millions. Stocks and mutual funds are trading at the highest levels in history. There are today more than twice as many Americans in the stock market as there were only 10 years ago. Every month, on average, another $11 billion is withdrawn from savings accounts and other safe investments and reinvested in the most speculative stock market the world has ever seen.

Neophyte investors are responsible for more than 80 percent of the $2.5 trillion invested in mutual funds over the past four years.

What that all means, statistically speaking, is that those who are the most at risk are the same ones who can least afford to take a hit. That has the experts worried.

> Sky-is-falling predictions tend to grab news headlines about the economic impact of the potential failure to adequately prepare the world's computers for the next millennium. "<u>The year-2000 issue will be the final blow to the bull market,</u>" year-2000 consultant Dennis Grabow told *The National Journal*. "<u>Let's stop pretending that Y2K</u> (geek-speak for year 2000) <u>isn't a major threat to our way of life</u>," Edward Yardeni, chief economist of Deutsche Bank Securities for North America, told a *Wall Street Journal* reporter. Some analysts warn that computer mishaps related to the millennium change could lead to a global recession, telecommunications breakdowns, and power outages. Some step out even further on the diving board, warning of possible malfunctions in systems that control nuclear weapons, and a federal government seriously impeded, with Medicare,

Social Security and veterans' payments stopped and air traffic halted. "I think there will be substantial dislocations in the US," said John Westergaard, president of Westergaard Year 2000, a publisher of webzines that analyze year-2000 issues. "There will be maybe an 80-percent reduction in air traffic at some time," he said. "I'm going to recommend to the Senate that an emergency hospital financing corporation be established to provide emergency financing to hospitals because the whole flow of Medicare reimbursement will come to a halt."[61]

Programming experts are divided into two groups—the optimists and the pessimists. A recent poll of the optimistic Y2K experts said 84 percent believe the bug will trigger the following;

- isolated supply breakdowns, like fuel, food or electricity.
- a 20 percent drop in the market.
- runs on banks.
- mild recession.

Y2K is a *global* threat—we can't emphasize that enough! The Millennium Bug is an equal

---

61 *Fox News,* July 1, 1998.

opportunity destroyer of data, and we live in a
world of international interconnectivity. One noncompliant system or even a single noncompliant
chip could begin spewing out inaccurate data that
could corrupt every system to which it is linked.

In Sweden, officials are already developing
contingency plans for what is anticipated to be a
total failure of their nuclear power grid. Nuclear
power furnishes about half of Sweden's electricity. This kind of situation corresponds roughly to
the *Brownout Scenario* we discussed earlier.

> Swedes may get an unwelcome foretaste of
> their plan to phase out nuclear power by
> 2010 unless computer experts crush the
> Millennium Bug. Sweden's nuclear watch-
> dog is tightening its grip on the power
> industry's 2000 preparations after uncover-
> ing a fault at an atomic unit which could
> have left many Swedes in the cold and the
> dark. Nuclear power workers are in for a
> dull and sober New Year 2000 as plants
> plan full staffing in case of problems. And
> some plants are worried the Millennium
> Bug might even strike at the end of this
> year. Maintenance personnel at the three-
> reactor Forsmark station sounded the
> alarm in July when they found that the
> plant's data system was unable to recognize

<u>the first two digits of the number 2000, resulting in an automatic shutdown.</u> "If possible millennium problems are not taken care of well in advance, people could face a cool and dark New Year's Eve," spokesman Anders Bjoerle at Sweden's nuclear power inspectorate (SKI) told Reuters. SKI has said it might order a temporary shutdown on the eve of the millennium and go over to hydro-power as a backup if it cannot guarantee there will be no computer problems. Bjoerle said SKI's first step was to inspect Sweden's 12 nuclear units, which produce around 50 percent of the country's total output. Testing has shown that the Millennium Bug could <u>prove fatal to nuclear power production.</u>[62]

But there are strong proponents among IT professionals for something a little closer to our *Blackout Scenario.* They expect:

• strong recession, local social disruptions and many business bankruptcies, at best, to,
• depression, market collapse, martial law, and the collapse of the US government at worst.

---

62 *Reuters News Service*, August 18, 1998.

Those are the opinions of those who are supposed to fix the problem. And, the experts are beginning to admit they can't fix it in time. The organizer of the bug fixit group is Bruce Webster. He told *Newsweek* in May 1998, "The longer people work in this area, the more pessimistic they are that it can be fixed." And Webster's own view of what will happen when the clock strikes 12:00? He believes the worst case scenario is the most likely.

The federal government collects more data on year-2000 readiness than does private industry. US businesses have no central clearing house for information on year-2000 compliance. In November, Senator Robert Bennett, R-Utah, introduced legislation that would require publicly traded companies to disclose their year-2000 progress in initial offering statements and in quarterly reports. The Securities and Exchange Commission now is demanding more disclosure of year-2000 spending in company reports. The New York Stock Exchange has used surveys to determine the readiness of member firms, brokers and other parties, NYSE Chairman Richard Grasso told a Senate committee in April. Roach said that the absence of data makes it impossible to predict the impact on financial markets of a widespread failure to prepare for the year 2000. "There is no data that would enable you to predict with any degree of confidence, in my opinion, a Y2K recession," he said. "It's not a conventional, easily measurable issue."[63]

But judge for yourself. If there's a danger that a bug will wipe out computer records on January 1, where will you have your money? Will it be in the bank? Or the stock market? Or will it be in cash under your mattress? And, if that's how <u>you</u> are going to protect your life savings, <u>what do you think everybody else is going to do</u>? (*Retiring Federal Reserve spokesman Joseph Coyne left his manual typewriter behind for computer users, saying, "It's the Year 2000 contingency plan."* We know where he'll have his.)

63 *Fox News*, July 1, 1998.

Chapter Eight

TOWARD A NEW(ER) WORLD ORDER

Some Success Story!

+ + +

We've already taken a look at American preparedness (and the lack of it) for post-Millennial Midnight. By and large, it's a pretty dismal picture. The Y2K report card for the US federal government is a resounding F overall, despite those few high-profile agencies that look like they just might make it.

A typical federal success story—and one the government likes to talk about a lot—is Social Security.

The Social Security Administration gets high marks for being the most proactive of the federal agencies. It began working on a solution to its Year 2000 problem back in 1989, before most of us even knew there *was* a problem. Consequently, the SSA scored high marks on the General Accounting Office's Year 2000 Readiness Test. So, come what may, Social Security recipients can count on their checks being delivered without interruption across the century divide, right? Wrong.

The Social Security Administration doesn't actually issue payments. Social Security compiles a list of eligible beneficiaries each month, drawing on its database containing information on every single taxpayer in America—even the dead ones.

One of the authors typed his father's name into an Internet search engine. Within seconds, a Social Security database retrieved his name, dates of birth and death and his Social Security number, even though he has been dead for more than a quarter century.

This information prompts a whole new field of Y2K speculation. Would a noncompliant computer system's interpretation of the date mean that he's alive again? If so, would his name show up on the eligibility list again?

That list, once compiled by SSA, is forwarded to another government agency called the Financial Management Service, a sub-agency of the US Treasury Department. The FMS is the agency which is actually responsible for the issuing of benefit checks or making direct deposits to beneficiaries.

According to Treasury Secretary Robert Rubin, the Treasury Department is in pretty good shape for Y2K compliance overall. There is only one sub-agency with truly serious compliant problems. You guessed it. The only Treasury Department agency whose ability to function past Millennial Midnight is in doubt is the Financial Management Service. The FMS is the agency charged, not only with the actual disbursement of SSA benefits, but also with the financial transactions of a significant portion of virtually every government agency.

This is another example of the hidden consequences of Y2K, even if *almost* all the systems are ready in time. Social Security has been working on the problem for the last decade. They're on time, and ready to face the challenges of the new millennium. They can do everything on the other side of the century mark that they can do now. Except issue checks.

The Global Report Card

+ + +

Because we are Americans, it is natural that we look at Y2K from an American perspective. Consequently, we think in terms of how Y2K will affect the American banking system, the US domestic power grid, or US federal agencies like Social Security, the Veteran's Administration, or the Internal Revenue Service.

The danger in such thinking is that it presents an incomplete picture, given the realities of the Global Village. If it looks like most of America's noncompliant mission critical systems will be fixed in time (highly unlikely, but within the realm of distant possibility) then we may not have too much to worry about, right? Maybe, like the Tylers, we'll have at least the basic necessities restored in a matter of a few days or a week. In that case, maybe Y2K *will* just be a temporary inconvenience.

It's an attractive thought and therefore hard to resist. Even as we wade through the research available on the subject, sifting through raw data that supports a scenario much worse than we presented for the Tylers, we still have trouble really *believing* it all—it's just too incredible to take in. As we sit in front of our computer monitors, typing this manuscript on functional computers in well lit rooms, sipping on coffee kept warm by desktop warmer plates, filtering out the background sounds of life in the late 20th century, it's hard to imagine that it could all simply vanish at the stroke of midnight.

America's report card is dismal, rating an overall "F" from the General Accounting Office. This is in spite of the many federal agencies whose Y2K preparations will be completed in advance of the deadline. Compared to some of the other major industrialized nations, however, America is way out in front in its efforts to minimize the effect of the Millennium Bug.

Missing the Point
+ + +

If you think that fixing America's computers means America has nothing to worry about from Y2K, then you've missed the point. The only way to totally squash the bug is to fix every computer on earth before January 1, 1999, and conduct a full year's live testing program.

Obviously, we're not going to make it, but even if we did, the only way to maintain our computer network integrity would be to seal the borders electronically. That is, we would have to sever any computer network connections that link a compliant American computer with a non-compliant foreign system. Assistant Secretary of Defense John Hamre explained why in testimony before Congress back in April 1996.

> "The management aspects associated with the Year 2000 are a real concern. With our global economy and the vast electronic exchange of information among our systems and databases, the timing of coordinated changes in date formats is critical. Much dialogue will need to occur in order to prevent a 'fix' in one system from causing another system to 'crash.' If a system fails to properly process information, the result could be the corruption of other databases, extending perhaps to databases in other government agencies or countries. Again, inaction is simply unacceptable; coordinated action is imperative."

To paraphrase, if a compliant computer sends compliant data in a compliant format to another computer, this transfer may crash that computer.

Or the recipient computer may not recognize the compliant format. In either case, the whole system breaks down.

Just as obvious as the fact we aren't going to make it in time is the fact we can't "seal the borders" to electronic communication. Efforts to censor offensive material on the World Wide Web has demonstrated the impossibility of such a task. The only way to censor the Internet is to shut it down completely. It is also the only way to seal America's electronic borders to foreign infection. And, that's not going to happen.

That means that, for America to escape the impact of Y2K, the whole world has to be ready in time. For example, the world's central banks are all linked to the Federal Reserve's computer network system, and to each other. If the central bank computer in, say Moscow, was noncompliant, then the corrupted information it transmits to the Fed's computer would be replicated throughout the global banking system in a matter of seconds. Would that mean that every computer on that network would have to start over at square one? Nobody knows for sure, but it's possible. So, how's the rest of the world doing on their own bug eradication projects, and what threat do their programs, or lack of them, represent to the United States?

Who's Afraid of a Little Bug?

+ + +

Russia has the world's second largest arsenal of nuclear weapons and perhaps a dozen decaying nuclear reactors. No one appears to know what will happen when the clocks on aging Soviet-era computers that control them click over from 1999 to 2000. More than that, nobody really seems to care. With problems like famine, epidemic disease, an economic collapse, and the unfilled political vacuum left behind by the former Soviet Union, Russia already has enough on its plate and can't find the time to take on something as expensive as fixing Y2K.

Analysts say Russia's most vulnerable systems are in its aging nuclear plants and defense systems. Information about those computers is secret, and predictions about whether failures can be expected are varied and probably unreliable. One thing is clear. The people who oversee these sectors don't seem concerned. A Defense Ministry spokesman, who refused to give his name, said he knew about the Millennium Bug. As for the ministry's efforts, he gave a Soviet-style response: "We're working on it, but I can't give you the details." In June, US Deputy Defense

Secretary John Hamre told a congressional hearing in Washington that he was concerned Russia had no program for determining whether its "fragile" nuclear missile early warning system might be crippled by the bug. Igor Sergeyev, Russia's defense minister, was asked about the issue during a news conference in August. His answer was nothing short of confusing. "This problem mostly affects sectors where they use conventional computer technologies. There is no such danger, since in the Strategic Missile Forces we use special technologies," he said, without offering details. An errant missile launch against the United States brought on by a computer clock failure would be highly improbable because Russia's nuclear weapons can't be unleashed by machines alone. But computer snags could gum up related systems, such as radar and telecommunications networks, said Ron Piasecki, an American consultant who has worked extensively with the US government on the Millennium Bug.[64]

---

64 "Year 2000 Computer Glitch a Russian Low Priority," AP, September 15, 1998.

Sergeyev says that Y2K presents no problem because Russia uses what he calls "special technologies." We would advise that you don't bet the farm on that statement. It's just a smokescreen designed to mask the problem, which the Kremlin sees as far lower on its priority list than issues like impending famine, imminent economic collapse, and a descent into anarchy. The Kremlin finds itself in a "catch-22" situation. It can't look to the IMF for help unless it cuts spending to meet IMF guidelines, and it can't cut spending if it tackles the Y2K bug. It's a choice between the devil and the deep blue sea; fix Y2K and face imminent economic collapse as a result now, or ignore Y2K and face economic collapse as a result of Y2K. Like most politicians, Russia's lawmakers prefer to let the next crop of elected officials face the music later, so they can make hay now.

In order for Russia to steady its tumbling economy via the IMF loans, it must drastically reduce government spending. This reduction in spending for the sake of preserving its fledgling capitalist economy could end up destroying it. Y2K induced failures resulting from inadequate preparation could cripple this already limping country, making the IMF bailout loans a moot point. Russia is possibly the most backward industrialized nation when it comes to Y2K remediation. It wasn't until May of this year that Prime Minister Sergei Kiriyenko instructed government agencies to examine themselves for possible Y2K problems. Until that time, Russia had adopted a wait and see policy of Y2K remediation in which the government would not begin work on Y2K susceptible systems until the problems sprang up, after January 1, 2000. The reasoning behind this cavalier philosophy was based on the fact that the government uses fewer computers than its Western counterparts, and that these systems were designed differently, a fact that supposedly made them impervious to the Millennium Bug.[65]

The argument that Russia is less susceptible than the West is to Y2K is patently foolish, as we've already discovered, thanks to the cascade effect. The two most heavily computerized segments of Russia's infrastructure are the banking and finance industry, and Russia's nuclear weapons arsenal.

To many familiar with the situation in Russia, news of this approach to Y2K is

---

65 "Russia and Its Vulnerability to Y2K," John Yellig, *Westergaard 2000,* July 17, 1998.

terrifying. The thought of the devastating effects a nationwide Russian computer shutdown could have on world financial markets is easily forgotten when the danger posed by nuclear weapons whose computers crash is considered. With one of the largest nuclear weapons arsenals in the world, many believe that Russia is in no position to be taking chances with their computers failing. Rumors abound of a program written into Russian ICBMs (Inter-Continental Ballistic Missiles) that automatically launches them when no one has interfaced with their central computer in a set period of time. Many believe that when the millennium rolls over, the computers will think that it has been almost 100 years since they were last accessed and immediately launch the entire battery of nuclear weapons to different destinations around the world.[66]

The *only* special technology that will insulate Russia against the ravages of Y2K would be a computer network designed from inception to

---

66 "Russia and Its Vulnerability to Y2K," John Yellig, *Westergaard 2000,* July 17, 1998.

use a four-digit year-date code. Since most of Russia's technology was either stolen from the West or reverse engineered from Western software, it is as susceptible to the Y2K bug as we are. Russian claims of "special technology" are reminiscent of the Cold War, when Russia claimed that it invented everything from television to shoelaces.

> Still, for a country with so many sensitive computer systems, Russia has no systematic plan of attack. The commission's checklist, for example, primarily helps government agencies understand how vulnerable they are. It doesn't tell them what to do about it. Russian businesses also seem to be moving slowly. In a survey of 50 Russian companies by the international consulting firm Coopers and Lybrand, only a third said they were even aware of the problem. Some Russians believe the nation's financial and banking systems are better off than those in the West because the Russian computers are more up-to-date than many of those running Western exchanges.[67]

---

67 "Russia and Its Vulnerability to Y2K," John Yellig, *Westergaard 2000*, July 17, 1998.

Denial Is Not a River in Egypt

+ + +

Russians have an incredible capacity for self-delusion when it comes to Russian technology versus anything Western. For 70 years, the Russian people believed they were locked in a neck and neck race with the West in the research and development of all the latest technologies. It wasn't until after the collapse of the Soviet Union that Russians got their first look inside an American supermarket and discovered that it was, in reality, a third world country. Russians thought their space program was way ahead of NASA, until they saw Cape Canaveral up close. They believed their weapons systems were superior until the Persian Gulf War proved otherwise.

Until 1991, most people behind the Iron Curtain thought black and white vacuum tube televisions were state of the art and that having two different television stations was the last word in entertainment.

For 70 years, reality in Russia was what the government decreed to be reality. Old habits die hard; so, when the Russian government announces it has "special technology" that will defeat Y2K, few people question that assessment.

Because of the Russian propensity to extol the virtues of all things Russian and to discount the capabilities of the West, most Russians are either unaware or unconcerned about the potential dangers. Indeed, two thirds of Russia's 50 largest companies think the best way to deal with the Millennium Bug is to spray it liberally with insecticide, if they see one scurrying around their computer.

What About Japan?

+ + +

After the United States, Japan is probably the most technically advanced society on the face of the earth. Japan has been on the cutting edge of technological advancement, particularly in the areas of computers and electronic computing devices, for as long as such devices have been in existence. If you have a typical American household, most of the electronic devices in your home carry brand names like Sony, Mitsubishi, Hitachi, Kenwood or Panasonic.

Japan is a miracle nation of sorts, having emerged from the ashes of World War II as one of the world's leaders in electronics research and development. If there were any nation on earth that should be able to grasp the dangers presented by Y2K, it should be the Japanese.

At least, you'd think so. The Tokyo Stock Exchange admitted in August 1998 that less than

10 percent of 1,549 companies that responded to a recent survey said they had completed their Millennium Bug preparations. A government report recommended that Japanese companies should set a deadline of June 1, 1999, to complete necessary Y2K repairs.

It's an ambitious project, considering that 90 percent of Japanese industry has yet to complete repairs. Unfortunately, there isn't enough time, so the June 1 deadline will come and go and repairs will still not be completed. Even if every company in Japan somehow does meet the June 1 deadline, that doesn't mean that Japan will have licked the Y2K problem. As we've already pointed out, it takes a full year of testing to ensure that every date in every program is compliant. Tokyo's deadline only makes provisions for six months of testing, not nearly enough time to iron out all the wrinkles.

In other words, even in the best of worlds—one in which every computer system in the whole country is Y2K compliant by June 1, 1999, it won't be good enough to squash the Bug. Put into even fewer words, Japan's compliance program is hopelessly inadequate to the task at hand. The Bug will bite, and bite hard, and the sting will be felt from Tokyo to New York.

Dragon Their Feet

+ + +

Most of the so-called "dragon nations" of Asia are already falling behind schedule in their Y2K remediation efforts.

"Among Asian countries, only Taiwan, South Korea and Singapore feature in Gartner's Level 2 readiness list, and <u>none</u> made it to Level 1 readiness," Duggan said. Level 2 readiness indicates a predicted Y2K-related mission-critical failure among 33 percent of a country's companies, while Level 1 denotes that 15 percent of a nation's companies are expected to suffer a Y2K-related mission-critical failure.

Asian countries in Level 3 (50 percent failure) include India, Malaysia, North Korea, and, importantly, Japan, Duggan said (at the Y2K Bug: Threat to Business Community conference). "Because of the size and importance of its economy, Japan's lack of Y2K readiness could cause major problems to ripple out," he said.

Also important is the presence of China in Level 4, where 66 percent of companies are expected to suffer a mission critical failure. China's extensive and growing trade links could cause Y2K problems for its neighbors, Duggan said. The remaining Asian countries in Level 4 include Cambodia, Indonesia, Laos, Pakistan, the Philippines, Thailand, and Vietnam.[68]

But although most corporate and government systems are far behind, Asia's banking industry is moving forward despite the obstacles thrown up by Asia's economic depression.

Banks in the Philippines, Korea, Australia, the mainland, New Zealand, Thailand, and Malaysia are expected to fix the Bug this year, a Reuters survey has found. Singapore banks were required to convert their systems to Y2K-compliance by the end of December, the Merrill Lynch report said. Hong Kong, Japan, India, Bangladesh, Taiwan and Sri Lanka say they expect bank compliance to be completed by next year. Few banks in Pakistan have on-line systems, so the issue there is more pressing for foreign institutions. Indonesia's local banks are struggling just to survive, much less to achieve compliance. Spending money to become compliant has not been easy. Banks

---

68 "Japan, China Face Y2K Crunch," *ComputerWorld NewsWire,* November 13, 1998.

<u>in Asia are battling deteriorating asset qual-
ity, fresh capital needs, and huge losses.</u>[69]

According to the *South China Morning Post,*
although Beijing is taking the threat of Y2K seriously, much of the population is complacent,
believing, like so many others, that Y2K only
presents a problem to those industries that are
heavily computerized.

"The chairman of the China Computer
Industry Association, Zhang Qi, said it was
dangerous to think the mainland could
escape the Bug, known as Y2K, because
computers were not widely used. Many of
the country's important sectors, such as
national defense, the financial industry,
and posts and telecommunications, already
depend on computer networks to operate,
and will, in turn, be affected by the Y2K
problem. While the People's Bank of
China, the Civil Aviation Administration of
China and some other organizations had
started to tackle the problem, <u>other departments had not paid much attention to it</u>.
Asia's banks could prove the only bright
spot on the slim list of industries whose

---

69 Reuters (Singapore), August 13, 1998.

computers are prepared to deal with the Year 2000 problem, government officials and analysts say. With their energies focused on dealing with the region's economic crisis, many companies have been distracted from fixing the so-called "Millennium Bug," a computer problem that arises because many systems fail to recognize the date for the year 2000.[70,71]

Panic in the Streets

+ + +

The problem with Y2K doesn't end with repairing the programming. We've already discussed the danger of linking a noncompliant computer to one that has been upgraded.

This analogy might help. If a healthy person walks into a tuberculosis ward, what happens? Do all the infected people catch "health" from the healthy person? Or, does the person without the infection eventually get sick? The same analogy holds for computers. Linking a "healthy" computer to a "sick" computer equals *two* "sick" computers and *no* healthy ones.

---

70 *South China Morning Post,* August 13, 1998.
71 See endnotes for Y2K Readiness Predictions by Country and Industry.

Even if every computer on earth received the proper updating, there will still be panic in the streets come millennium time. A panic *will* happen as people recognize that the Y2K bug hasn't been fixed and that planes that happen to be airborne at 12:01 AM on January 1, 2000, will have a difficult time landing—if they don't simply plummet from the sky. As people begin to stockpile food, available supplies will dwindle. Even the perception of a shortage is enough to trigger panic buying, which will further exacerbate the situation as available supplies get even harder to find as a result.

A greater problem could be seen in the financial industry. People who fear automatic teller machines won't work after 2000—or that bank computers will forget their balances—might begin making early withdrawals just to ensure they have enough money on hand to live in the new millennium.

Although it's a good idea, for somebody to win, somebody else has to lose. The first ones to demand their money in cash won't have a problem. They win. But, eventually, the banks will run out of cash money and the doors will close. If you are standing in line when that happens, you lose.

The Federal Reserve is making contingency plans to ensure there will be enough cash available to meet the expected demand. At least, that's the view intended for public consumption. The Fed can't prevent what is to come, but it can at least try and calm public fears for as long as it can to postpone the moment of truth.

The Federal Reserve, as part of its Year 2000 plans, will be ready if Americans want to hold more cash than usual on New Year's Eve 1999, board governor Edward W. Kelley Jr. said at a Houston economic symposium last week. "We will be prepared to lend whatever sums may be needed . . . to provide needed reserves to the banking system," Kelley said. Experts fear that some people may want to keep more cash on hand because of concerns that computers might malfunction on January 1, 2000, and freeze their accounts or make business dealings difficult. Based on current projections, Fed officials expect to put from $30 billion to $50 billion in extra cash into inventories in late 1999 to ensure money can be made available to bank customers. Kelley suggested the nation will face "isolated production problems and disruptions to commerce" but said "the Y2K shock . . . is most likely to be short-lived and fully reversed." Kelley described himself as "cautiously optimistic that the Millennium mistic” that Y2K *won’t* cause “<u>major</u> economic dis-

Bug will not cause major economic disruptions when it bites.”[72]

Despite Governor Kelley’s earnest efforts to
minimize the danger, he couldn’t quite bring himself to say there is nothing to worry about. Instead,
he predicts “isolated” production and commerce
disruption. At best, he is only “cautiously optimistic” that Y2K *won’t* cause “<u>major</u> economic disruptions.” His comments are most noteworthy for
what he *didn’t* say. Kelley *didn’t* say he was optimistic there would be *no* economic disruptions,
but rather, that he anticipated no *major* disruptions. Still, he sees Y2K coming as a “shock” that is
only “likely” to be short-lived and fully reversed.”

One of the reasons for his caution is the fact
that when the first shock comes, it will come when
depositors find out they don’t actually have any
money in the bank. The total amount of money
people *think* is in their checking and savings
accounts amounts in total to some $3.7 trillion.
The *actual* <u>cash on reserve</u> in banks comes to only
$43.2 billion. That means, on average, for every
dollar you *think* you have in the bank, the bank
has, on average, about 17 cents! If every depositor
demanded his or her deposits in cash at the same

72 “Fed Plans for Cash Reserves,” *Washington Post,*
November 5, 1998.

time, then your $10,000 withdrawal slip would only be worth $1700. The only thing maintaining the fiction that our economy is built on is the confidence that our money will be there when we want it. That fiction will be exposed in short order if and when Y2K prompts a bank "run." And Fed Governor Edward Kelley knows it.

Millennium Madness?
+ + +

On the other side of the equation are those who pooh-pooh Y2K as just another example of "Millennium Madness." You've heard them, no doubt, patiently explaining that something like this happens every millennium.

There is precedence for this sort of behavior. Every now and then, some religious seer will gather a group of faithful, max out all their credit cards and wait for the big day. Others simply latch onto a comet and fly away. As the first millennium approached, people went crazy, too. Figuring something big was about to happen, a lot of them quit caring for their homes, left their crops in the fields and basically quit working altogether. And they didn't have credit cards to abuse, or it could've gotten really ugly.[73]

---

73 Editorial, *The Memphis Business Journal,* September 14, 1998.

They didn't have something else back then, either, a crucial something necessary to make the Millennium Madness theory work. They didn't have printing presses, and what little documentary evidence we have for social conditions as they existed in AD 1000 say very little about the global reaction to the approaching millennium. The last millennium was a thousand years ago. The Crusaders were still trying to capture Jerusalem from the Muslims. The Battle of Hastings was still 66 years into the future. The *Magna Carta* wouldn't be signed for more than 200 years. Conventional wisdom said the earth was flat, and that piece of "science" formed the foundation for the principles of navigation for the next 500 years, until "1492, when Columbus sailed the ocean blue."

A thousand years ago, Europeans believed that bathing was injurious to health and that illnesses could be cured by casting spells.

A historian could examine any 12-month period for 100 years on either side of the millennium and conclude that the population was suffering from "millennial madness," but only if he applied contemporary Western values to ancient civilization. And that would be nonsense, not history. The main difference between the way we see the new millennium and the way our ancestors did is colored by

1000 years of scientific and technical advancement. The "Millennial Madness" theory has to ignore that fact or collapse under its own weight.

Y2K is not a manifestation of some weird collective insanity. Y2K is the result of shortsighted computer programmers who forgot that 2000 follows 1999. We'd prefer to believe that this millennium will pass like the last one, with all the dire predictions being nothing more than ignorant superstition. Unfortunately for us, Y2K is as real as a punch in the nose. And, in the long run, infinitely more painful.

Going Global
+ + +

Y2K is a global problem, and the most efficient way to attack a global problem is by employing a global solution. That will undoubtedly involve the United Nations. And while a global solution seems like the most logical approach, it is shot full of hidden dangers.

To attack Y2K, a global authority must be able to take charge of the Y2K problem. That sentence encapsulates the danger of a global solution. First, to *be* a global authority, you have to *have* authority. That means turning control of the world's infrastructure over to *somebody*. That's what being "in charge" is all about.

Let's Get Gorby!

+ + +

There are plans in the works to appoint such a czar. A recent Year 2000 computer conference in Washington, DC, featured the developer of many of the computer codes now in use, including ASCII and COBOL, Robert Bemer.

The conference was called, appropriately, "Drastic Measures for Drastic Times" and Bemer was certainly on topic. In his keynote speech, Bemer called on the United States to support the appointment of an all-powerful Y2K czar with the authority to force every nation on earth to put Y2K at the top of its priority list, and supervise and monitor compliance efforts.

It sounds like a reasonable idea, on the surface. Until you look closely at the potential ramifications of such a move. Bemer's nominee for the job is former Soviet premier Mikhail Gorbachev.

Gorby has been looking for an opportunity to take over *something*—in recent years he has been active in the environmental movement, but now he has a government job. Gorbachev is now Russia's Y2K "awareness" spokesman. (Although judging from the state of Russia's preparedness, he's not doing a very good job.) Bemer thinks that he'd be just perfect for King of the Keyboard, and he's not alone. Back on October 17, 1997, Representative Stephen Horn's congressional committee investigating Y2K called just one expert witness. That "expert" was Mikhail Gorbachev.

So, once the nations of the world have agreed to allow a single authority to coordinate repairs and upgrades and to enforce compliance issues, whether it is Gorbachev, or someone else, what do we do when Y2K is all over? Do we fire the global czar? Who fires him? What if he doesn't *want* to be fired?

Consider the following scenario. The US decides it no longer wants to be under the authority of a global cyber-cop. But the majority of the members of the UN disagree. The US decides to go it alone and just opt out of the agreement.

Suddenly, the American infrastructure collapses and it's like Y2K all over again, only this time, it isn't random brownouts, but a full scale, planned blackout! How long do you think it would take before we cried "uncle"?

Sounds Familiar, Somehow!

+ + +

The creation of some kind of agency that could oversee Y2K conversion on a global scale seems like the smart move. Maybe too smart.

Whoever headed that agency would be the King of the Keyboard in a wired world. And like it or not, we would all be his subjects. The whole scenario has an eerily familiar ring to it.

In the book of the Revelation, chapter 13, the Apostle John describes a coming world government headed by a single individual called the "beast." John says that beast has unique powers so great that the cry goes up, "Who is like unto the beast, and who is able to make war with him?" Certainly, if the "beast" has the ability to turn off a nation's light switches at will to enforce policy, the answer would be nobody. How would America—or any other country, for that matter—be able to march against an enemy half a world away after being plunged, electronically, back into the middle of the 19th century?

John goes on to describe another characteristic of the "beast" in verse 17. He says, "And he causeth all, small and great, free and bond, to accept a mark in their right hand or in their forehead. And that no man might buy or sell unless he has the mark, or the name of the beast, or the number of his name."

Never in history was it possible for any single individual to control commerce on such an intimate scale. Before the advent of the computerized global economy, that is. Today, all that is necessary to fulfill John's prophecy is someone to sit at a master keyboard and punch in a few keystrokes. So far, there is no master keyboard and no *one* person who can punch in the right combination of keystrokes on it.

Y2K may change all that. Whether we like it or not.

Chapter Nine

THINKING THE UNTHINKABLE

hat Y2K is a global menace is undeniable, at this point. The degree to which it will affect our heavily wired world is predicated by the cascade effect. Predicting exactly how all the elements will interact would be something akin to predicting human history. To predict the life of someone like Adolf Hitler or Josef Stalin, you would have to know—in advance—that Josef Stalin's great-great-grandmother would decide to marry his great-great-grandfather, rather than choosing, for example, to enter a convent. If *that* happened, then Josef Stalin would arguably have never existed. The same applies in the life of Adolf Hitler. That would mean that their collective millions of victims may have lived full lives, raised children, who would *also* have affected the course of history in ways we can only imagine. How many Albert Einsteins, Stephen Hawkings, Bill Gates or Ronald Reagans perished in the 1930s and 1940s on the orders of these men? What would our world be like today if there had been no Einsteins, Hawkings, Gates or Reagans at all? Consider the effect each of these men had on science, technology, and society. Imagine if humanity had the benefit of the talents of all those who were lost?

The point is, each generation had a cascade effect on the generation that followed. The advances made in any single generation are interdependent on the generation before.

That same interdependence, or cascade effect, is what makes predicting exactly how Y2K will affect the global computer network impossible. The best we can do is make educated guesses based on the knowledge available to us at this point in time, in the waning weeks of 1998.

For example, will the power grid go down, or just the telephone system? Obviously, if the power grid goes down as well, it will take much longer to get the rest of the infrastructure rebooted, because you can't even begin until electricity is restored. On the other hand, even if the basic infrastructure survives, will billing snafus so snarl the business community that small and medium size companies will go bankrupt as their cash flow dries up? Will the cascade effect of corporate bankruptcies trigger a recession, or a full blown depression? What about utilities? Will your electricity supplier's Y2K-intoxicated computer system disconnect your service when you fail to pay a bill for $111,234.894.36 for service from 31/12/99 to 31/01/00?

The point is that, due to the unpredictability of the cascade effect, we don't know how bad it's actually going to be. We do know one thing for sure, however. Y2K is going to hit hard, and things are going to get bad. Beyond that, it's just a question of degrees.

What You Don't Know
<u>Will</u> Hurt You
+ + +

Many people don't know the difference between
Y2K *ready* and Y2K *compliant*. If you are among
those, then you are likely to be among those who
will feel the Bug's bite early. There is a world of
difference between the two terms, as we pointed
out in Chapter One. To save you looking it up
again, NERC (North American Electricity
Reliability Council) summarizes the difference
between the two:

> Y2K Ready means a system or component
> has been determined to be suitable for
> continued use into the Year 2000. Note
> that this is not necessarily the same as Y2K
> Compliant, which implies fully correct
> date manipulations.

Understanding the difference between the
two terms, taken to the extreme, *could* be an issue
of life or death. Is the 747 jumbo jet you are rid-
ing on Y2K *ready*, or is it Y2K *compliant*? Are the
500 or so onboard computers that control everything from environmental control to navigation
and landing "suitable for continued use into the
Year 2000," or are they capable of "fully correct
date manipulations"? The subtle semantic differ-
ences between the two will make a big difference

as the clock approaches Millennial Midnight.

If you don't understand the difference between the two early on, you are just liable to put your faith in a social safety net that just might not be there to catch you when you need it most. Social Security, as we have already seen, got high marks from the Horn committee, who scored it A+. The SSA got that high score because it will be 100 percent Y2K *ready* by March 1999. Y2K *ready* is the best that any federal agency can manage. No system can be Y2K *compliant*, or, "capable of fully correct date manipulations" without a full year's live testing. You can't squeeze a year out of eight months, no matter how hard you try.

To be capable of fully correct date manipulations, a system has to be live-tested for each day of the year. A live test with simulations for the first three calendar months isn't a "live test" at all. It's a "modified" live test, which is the same kind of "double-speak" that George Orwell foresaw in his classic novel *1984*. A "modified live-test" is the same kind of haphazard temporary "patch" that gave birth to the Millennium Bug to begin with.

How's That Again?
+ + +

The government's "report card" is dismal, to be sure. But it is actually much worse than it appears to be. For example, Social Security is 99 percent of the way toward full "readiness" in 1999, before the clock changes. But notice the wording at the top of the chart which we will reprint for convenience on the opposite page.

There is a phrase there, *mission critical*. The term "mission critical" refers to those systems that are absolutely essential to maintaining minimum functionality. It doesn't refer to all the computer networks or desktop computers within a particular agency, but only those deemed to be the most critical to operations. In other words, the government report card is a carefully crafted document that painstakingly understates certain key points that would present a more accurate, but far more dismal outlook for the immediate post Y2K future. By separating out the mission critical computing systems [from, what, the *unnecessary* systems?] the report conceals one fact and ignores another. It conceals the fact that a great many of the computers that we use to maintain our federal infrastructure will not even be Y2K *ready* by Millennial Midnight, and it ignores the potential for re-infection of the "mission critical" systems from those systems unprepared for Y2K that fall outside that category.

Re-reading the government's readiness chart in that light paints a picture of a federal government without a *single* branch that is expected to be fully Y2K *compliant* by the turn of the century.

Mission Critical Systems
of Federal Departments and
Agencies

Year 2000 Progress—As of September 1998

Agency	Year Complete	By 3/99	Feb 98	May 98	Aug 98
Social Security	1999	99%	A	A+	A
National Science Foundation	1999	100%	A	A-	A
Small Business Admin	1999	98%	B	B	A
General Services	1999	91%	C	A-	B+
Commerce	1999	100%	B	B	B
EPA	1999	92%	B	B	B
VA	1999	88%	A	C	B-
FEMA	1999	92%	C	A-	B-
NASA	2000	74%	D	B	C+
Agriculture	1999	89%	B	D	C
HUD	1999	78%	B	C	C
Treasury	2000	61%	D	C	D+
DOT	1999	70%	F	F	D
Office of Personnel Mgt.	2000	65%	B	C-	D
DOD	2001	54%	F	D	D
Labor	2001	52%	F	C	D
Interior	2005	37%	C-	C-	D
Nuclear Reg. Commission	2001	43%	C-	B	D
Health & Human Svces	2002	48%	D	F	F
Dept of Energy	2002	47%	D-	F	F
Dept. of State	2027	37%	F	F	F
Dept. of Justice	2030+	31%	C-	D	F
Dept of Education	2030+	29%	F	D	F
Agency for Int'l Dev	2023	16%	D-	F	D
Administration Overall		66%	D-	F	D

Source: Congressional Subcommittee on Government Management, Information and Technology

Furthermore, by designating only *mission critical* systems into the equation, the report card conceals the real state of vulnerability within the federal infrastructure as a whole.

Mission critical is a term without definition, as we have already suggested. If there was a hard definition for "mission critical," then there would also be a way to define those systems that are redundant. No federal agency wants to suggest *any* of their equipment is redundant (that is the same as admitting it is unnecessary), so the scale slides back and forth. When justifying budgetary items, *all* systems are *"mission critical,"* but, for purposes of Y2K accountability, almost *none* of their systems is mission *critical*.

Kind of Critical, Anyway!

+ + +

For example, when the Pentagon sought funding for its more than 25,000 computer systems, they were *all* "critical." When pressed to quantify its Y2K remediation efforts, the Pentagon identified, out of those 25,000 systems, 3,143 systems that they said were "mission critical."

Can you imagine a budgetary hearing that goes like this?

Congressman: "Mr. Secretary, do you really need to spend $3 million of taxpayer money on these new computer systems?"

Secretary of Defense: "No sir, we don't really need them, but some of our desks seem pretty bare without nice, new big-screen monitors on them. The people over at Commerce are starting to make fun of us."

Congressman: "Well, alrighty, then!"

Not Another Conspiracy Theory!

+ + +

Is there some kind of high-level Y2K conspiracy? Well, yes—and no. In the purest sense of the word, one could argue a Y2K-related conspiracy of sorts designed to cover up the true nature of federal readiness for the new millennium. A "conspiracy" is, by definition, "An agreement between two or more persons to commit a crime or accomplish a legal purpose through illegal action."[74]

The purpose behind hiding the federal government's vulnerability to Y2K is a justifiable effort to prevent public panic—more than merely a "legal purpose"; indeed, it is government's *responsibility* to maintain public order.

Is deliberately understating the number of mission critical computers requiring Y2K remediation an "illegal action"? Or, is deliberately

---

74 *The American Heritage® Dictionary of the English Language, Third Edition,* copyright © 1992 by Houghton Mifflin Company. Electronic version licensed from INSO Corporation. All rights reserved.

overstating the number of systems necessary (which is the only other possible explanation for why the Pentagon has nearly 10 times as many computers as it claims it needs) an illegal action?

The Department of Defense claims it didn't even become aware of the Y2K problem until 1995! So, was there a conspiracy of silence by one government agency (Social Security, who began Y2K repairs in 1989) to keep another agency, (DOD) in the dark? And since the DOD is charged with America's defense, couldn't that conspiracy of silence be viewed as treasonous?

Or, could there be a simpler explanation, no less horrendous for the country, but easier to deal with in the short term? Let's try this one on for size. There is enough evidence readily available to the public on the subject of Y2K to fill a book! (You hold the evidence to support that statement in your hands right now!) The overwhelming majority of experts in and out of government admit the consequences of the Millennium Bug will be severe.

> "A US Senate committee on the Y2K computer problem said that the likelihood is increasing that electric utilities will fail to fix all their systems on time. Senator Robert Bennett of Utah and chairman of the committee said recently that Americans

should prepare for such potential wide-spread power outages in the early part of 2000. According to the president of the Y2K Solutions Group, Robert Roskind, 'The grid is made up of thousands of dereg-ulated electric companies, and no one's taking the oversight to make sure that it holds together. <u>If we lose power, the Y2K problem is manifested a hundredfold</u>.'"[75]

The Millennium Logic Bomb has the potential to do more than make computers think it is 1900. At Millennial Midnight, we may find our-selves reliving the 20th century all over again.

One of the foremost authorities on the Y2K bug is Peter de Jaeger. He is the founder of the Year 2000 Information Center—a think tank focused on the problem. As he sees it, "the only technology immune to Y2K is not connected to a power source."

De Jaeger quoted the chairman of the Congressional Year 2000 Panel, Senator Robert Bennett at a conference recently. Even the name of the conference had an ominous ring. It was called "The Y2K Crisis—A Global Ticking Time Bomb?"

75 *The JVI Update*, WWW Website
http://www.jvim.com/cgi-bin/update.cgi

This was hardly a conspiracist conference. Senator Bennett was the keynote speaker. According to Bennett, *"If today were December 31, 1999, and our systems were in the current state they are in today, tomorrow our economy worldwide would stop. It wouldn't grind to a halt. It would snap to a halt. You would not have dial tone tomorrow if tomorrow were January 1st, year 2000. You would not have air travel. You would not have Federal Express. You would not have the Postal Service. You would not have water. You would not have power. Because the systems are broken."*

With all the evidence available to them, how is it that the top planners of the Pentagon, whose every move is planned to the tiniest detail, were in the dark? Their best excuse is that they failed to find out about the biggest threat to national security in history until six years *after* the Social Security Administration had already *begun* to work on the problem?

There must be a Y2K cover-up conspiracy. Any other explanation would have to factor in an admission that America is led by the most bumbling, incompetent, shortsighted administration in history!

The federal Y2K "readiness report card," dismal as it is, is a tissue of lies that conceals far more than it reveals. The conspirators are not trying to *prevent* a panic—*that* will certainly come if Y2K impacts the country the way the experts believe it will. Instead, they are trying to *stall* the coming panic for as long as they can, hoping they can survive long enough to leave the next administration to pick up the pieces. It's a conspiracy, all right. Mostly, it's a conspiracy of cowardice.

The Technology Administration?

+ + +

One of the Clinton Administration's earliest campaign pledges was to be the "technology administration." The Clinton-Gore team launched a nationwide campaign to put computers in schools and wire up "every child in America" to the Internet.

To that end, President Clinton named Al Gore as the nation's Chief Computer Wizard in Charge. Together, they attended a photo-op session at a California school where they were photographed wiring up that school's computer network, as if they were the next Bill Gates-Paul Allen "whiz kid" team.

Vice-President Gore attended another photo-op where he stood in front of a mountain of paperwork that he proclaimed "government waste." His task, given him by the President, was to "reinvent" government. Most of his "reinvention"

efforts were directed toward increasing government dependence on computer technology. A
kind of hybrid environmentalism whereby computer hugging equaled tree hugging. By increasing digital dependence, we could save paper and
therefore save the rainforests, reverse global
warming, and put "earth in the balance," as his
pre-election tome suggested.[76]

How is it that these two "technical whiz kids,"
the Champions of the Digital Age, could have
"forgotten" to tip off the Cabinet that the country's infrastructure was in peril? Or, was the
whole "whiz kid" agenda an elaborate con job?

During the 1998 elections, President Clinton
was said to be "fascinated" by Internet coverage
of the mid-term elections. Aides joked that they
had to keep showing him how to navigate from
one site to the next. Until early 1998, the people
who keep track of such things noted that
President Clinton had addressed exactly 140
words on the subject of Y2K in the first six years
of his administration. In one memorable quote,
he said, "Americans need not worry about the
computer clock problem."

---

76 Al Gore published his view of environmentalism in
Earth in the Balance, in 1992. His views prompted President
Bush to dub him "the Ozone Ranger."

Direct and Kind of Stern!

+ + +

Vice President Gore appeared to have forgotten that he was named Chief Computer Wizard in Charge of the American technological revolution. When reminded, he took immediate action!

> The Clinton administration is increasingly worried that federal agencies will fail to rid their computers of the Year 2000 Bug, prompting Vice President Al Gore to put additional pressure on federal executives to step up their Year 2000 conversion efforts. The Office of Management and Budget has also recalculated the cost of federal efforts to combat the Year 2000 computer problem at $5.4 billion, the *Washington Post* reported. G. Edward DeSeve, acting deputy director for management at the Office of Management and Budget, told a gathering of federal information technology executives Wednesday that the administration had asked Congress for $3.25 billion in fiscal 1998 supplemental spending for Year 2000 fixes. The funds, if approved, would be available until 2001 . . . Gore met with executives from the seven agencies whose Y2K efforts are the furthest behind—the departments of Defense, Education,

Energy, Health and Human Services, State
and Transportation and the Agency for
International Development. OMB's most
recent quarterly report on Y2K progress
revealed that some agencies won't make
the administration's September 30 deadline
for completing systems renovations. At the
meeting, Gore asked each agency representative to commit to making Y2K fixes their
top priority. "<u>The Vice President was very
direct and kind of stern</u>," DeSeve said, not-
ing that Gore closely questioned the Health
and Human Services representative about
Medicare systems.[77]

Let's have a look at that again! The estimated
costs have risen to $5.4 billion, $3.5 *billion* more
than budgeted! Gore met with the *seven* agencies
furthest behind:

•Defense: The Defense Department is the
agency that will protect us from enemies
and guarantee our American way of life. It
will have to take a hiatus until 2001. They
got a "D" on their report card.
•Education: This is the agency the administration promised to computerize to help

77 *Gov Exec Daily Briefing,* September 3, 1998.

it prepare the next generation for the Information Age. They are expected to be ready to prepare our children for the challenges of the new millennium sometime around 2030 or beyond, when the current crop of students are in their forties. They get an "F. "

•Energy: This is the agency in charge of America's nuclear weapons production program. Sometime around 2002, they expect to be ready for 2000. "F"

•Health and Human Services: This is the agency responsible for making sure you *live* into the next millennium. And they'll be ready to *do* that in 2002. Try not to get sick until then, okay? "F"

•State and Transportation: The agency in charge of making sure Americans can travel safely abroad and efficiently at home will be back on the job about 2027. So, as long as you don't have to take a trip, or use the nation's transportation system to ship food and commodities for about *27 years*, Y2K won't present too difficult a challenge. At least, it shouldn't be any more complicated than the peace efforts in the Middle East or Bosnia, or American diplomatic missions in places like Russia or China. "F"

•Agency for International Development: This is the agency that fuels America's global economic interests. Some Y2K "doomsayers" suggest the Bug might trigger a recession, or even a depression. Don't be scared! The Agency for International Development will be ready to protect America's interests in the global economy for the 21st in 2023. So, if everyone will just hold Uncle Sam's place in line for about 23 years, America's economic future remains secure. Incredibly, they get a "D" on their report card!

The report card concerned the Chief Computer Wizard in Charge so much that he called a meeting to "ask" the assembled department heads to "commit" to making Y2K a number-one priority as of late September 1998! And he didn't just *ask*—he was "direct and kind of stern." Stern? Whew! We'll bet there'll be plenty of action, now!

And all it took to wake up the Chief Computer Wizard in Charge was the potential collapse of Western civilization.

Chapter Ten

NOW THAT YOU KNOW, NOW WHAT?

IF=THEN . . .

+ + +

More than any other feeling, as we research the vast destructive potential of the Millennium Bug, the feeling that we get is one of helplessness. *If* Y2K hits the power grid . . . *if* it cuts the transportation network, *if* it shuts down hospitals, *if* the economy is halted . . . *IF, IF, IF!*

There is a phrase in computer programming called "IF=THEN" that allows the computer to adjust to variables and still correctly process data. For example, a program might say something like "IF NO CDROM, THEN GOTO HDD" to enable a program to first check for a program on a CDROM drive to complete a particular transaction. If the system is unable to locate the required file(s) on a CDROM, the statement tells the computer to use the system's hard disk drive to search for or process the information involved. Without such a statement, failing to find the necessary information on a CDROM could cause the program to fail, and, in a worse case scenario, cause the system to "freeze" completely.

By definition, Y2K is an "IF" scenario. Unfortunately, we have no alternative "THEN" procedure built in as a fail-safe. For example, IF the power grid goes down, THEN what will you and your family do? IF the banking system collapses, THEN will you have any alternative method to get your hands on some cash? IF the transportation system goes down, THEN will you have some alternative plan for feeding your family until the crisis has run its course? IF you choose to accept the "non-event" scenario of Sally Katzen THEN what will you do in the event of Michael Hyatt's Blackout Scenario?

Finally, IF you ARE prepared and THEN the Y2K effect DOESN'T materialize, will you be better or worse off than IF you *aren't* prepared and THEN Y2K does wreak havoc on our technology driven society?

Obviously, none of the preparations for Y2K will *hurt* you. How can having a stockpile of emergency rations, a store of drinking water, and an alternative source of heat damage you? On the other hand, having no food, no water and no source of heat in the event of a Y2K disaster could be extremely damaging—even fatal! As we have repeated several times, Y2K is the most *predictable* catastrophe in history.

> "In the Millennium Bug, we have developed a technology equivalent to natural forces. If it is anywhere, it is everywhere," says G. K. Jayaram, chairman of Transformation

Systems of Princeton, New Jersey.
"Nowhere at any time in human history
has there existed such a problem."[78]

But all the advance warning in the world
won't be of any value at all unless you heed the
warning in time. You can be warned to "duck,"
but the warning itself won't protect you. You
actually have to duck for the warning to be of any
value. On January 1, 2000, either Y2K will create
one of the disaster scenarios, or it will simply be
a non-event.

Imagine for a second that you are a soldier on
the front lines of a battlefield. Incoming shells
begin to explode all around you. The rest of your
buddies dive into foxholes. You look around and
realize that none of the shells have actually *hit*
you. What is your reaction? Do you "duck," or
just assume that since none have landed where
you are now, that none will, so you need not take
cover?

There is a traditional military saying that is
appropriate here. "There are old soldiers, and
there are bold soldiers, but there are *no* old, bold
soldiers." To carry the analogy just a bit further,
because you haven't personally met up with the

78 *USA TODAY*, November 13, 1998, "More Than
Computers Vulnerable to Y2K."

enemy, do you venture out on patrol with an empty weapon? Not if you want to come back.

Would you ignore a tornado warning because you don't personally see the funnel cloud? Would you ignore a drinking water hazard alert because you couldn't *see* anything floating in your glass of tap water? Why do you buy winter clothes in the early fall while it's still warm outside? And what is the point in picking up next week's groceries when you aren't hungry right now?

Assess The Threat
+ + +

The first thing to consider when making preparations against a potential Y2K disaster is to make an assessment of how Y2K will impact you in your circumstances. Where you will be located at Millennial Midnight will color every subsequent Y2K preparedness decision you make. Make this decision *first* and plan accordingly. For example, preparing an alternative source to heat your home is less of an issue to residents of Los Angeles, California, than it would be to residents of Salamanca, New York, where the snow cover in the winter averages three feet or more. If the pumps shut down and the taps run dry, where will you get fresh drinking water? In LA, that's a real problem. Without irrigation, southern California is really a desert. On the other hand, people in Salamanca will be grumbling about having to shovel *their* alternative fresh water supply off the front steps.

A family living in a rural mountain area in Montana or in a small community in the country somewhere will have less to worry about from food riots than a big city resident. In cities like New York, Chicago, Los Angeles or Dallas, once the planes, trains and automobiles stop running, it will only take a few hours to clean out the supermarkets. Where would an apartment dweller in New York or Los Angeles plant a vegetable garden?

Big city apartment dwellers seldom know very many of their neighbors, whereas in some smaller communities, everybody knows everybody else. In making your survival plans, can you count on pooling your resources with the rest of the people in your neighborhood, or should you prepare to go it alone?

Making plans to defend your home and family against invaders in gang-infested areas of Los Angeles might be different than planning for home defense in a small rural town in Pennsylvania or North Carolina.

Where you live right now, what are your chances of survival if the local infrastructure (fire, police, water, heat, electricity and communications) is disrupted? How long could you hold on until those services are restored?

Planning is the key to survival. And there are only two possible scenarios. One is to plan for a disaster that may or may not materialize. In this scenario, you are "stuck" with a supply of food and water, alternative sources of heat and light, and some available cash that you won't need. After January, 1, 2000, if nothing happens, you can eat the food, drink the water, and put your cash back in the bank. Or leave it alone as a fail-safe against some other natural disaster like a hurricane, flood or tornado.

The other scenario involves betting the survival of you and your family against the development of a last minute, "silver bullet" program that will correct the Y2K programming bug in every affected computer system in the world. You have to wonder about the kind of mental processes that would result in someone gambling everything they have, including the lives of themselves and their families, on the programming ability of *people they never met*. Especially in light of the fact they are assessing those programmers' skills, sight unseen, *based on their ability to fix something most people don't even understand*. And there *are* people like that, hard as it seems to believe. If you doubt it, take a tour of Las Vegas, Nevada.

Assuming that you are one of those who feel their family is too important to risk on blind faith in luck alone, there are some things you can do. Assess the threat Y2K poses to you where you live. Imagine what it would be like one week after a worst-case Y2K disaster hits your community. In some cases, you might even consider packing up and moving somewhere safer, just in case. Exactly where you plan to be when the dominos begin to topple is the most important Y2K preparedness decision you will make. Even in the best possible Y2K scenario, John Sarazen, director of SynComm Group, a technology-consulting firm warns, "The sky isn't falling; there are just some chunks going to come down."[79] Whether or not some of those chunks land on you will depend on whether or not you are prepared to meet the threat.

How Long Will the Crisis Last?
+ + +

Like so many other things in the modern world, it depends on who you ask. In the most optimistic scenario, it is estimated that only eight percent of the potential Y2K related computer failures will occur at the stroke of midnight, January 1, 2000. The rest of the failures will occur over the following two years. That doesn't

---

79 USA TODAY, November 13, 1998, "The Truth About Y2K Myths."

sound too bad. Unless the systems among that eight percent are critical systems that control our basic infrastructure. Then those system failures will cascade through the system, as we have already seen. If the *only* computer system to fail is the one that controls the electric power grid, then how will we get it back on line? It's a chicken and egg problem; if the computer has to be repaired before the power goes back on, and you need power to turn *on* the computer to fix the defective programming, then how do you fix the computer? And until you fix the computer, how do you turn on the power?

And, even if the mainframes that control our power grid are not among the doomed eight percent, *that is only the beginning.* Over the two years that immediately follow Millennial Midnight, computer problems of all types will continue to snarl our information technology net.

As we've already seen, the federal government is nowhere near ready to face the Year 2000. The "peace, love and tranquilizers, have a nice day" scenario Sally Katzen tried to sell to the Congress may have lulled some Congressmen. It may have calmed the fears of the laymen who don't understand how computers work. But it hasn't fooled the experts.

"Nobody seems willing or able to say it in simple language, so let me be the one: *The federal government is not going to finish its Y2000 project.* No maybes, no ifs, ands or buts. No qualifiers, no wishy-washy statements like 'unless more money is spent' or 'unless things improve.' We're not going to avert the problem by appointing a Y2K czar or creating a National 2000 Commission. *Let me say it again, in plain English: The* United States government will NOT finish its Y2K project. . . . How Washington expects to keep functioning is a mystery to me. How American society expects to keep operating in a 'business as usual' fashion when half the federal government agencies stop functioning is a deeper mystery, and <u>one for which we should all begin planning.</u>"[80]

In the final analysis, how long Y2K lasts is anybody's guess, but nobody <u>knows for sure!</u> That is the reality. There are those who will mock preparation efforts, based on what they heard from this expert, or that one, but without ever realizing that the mere fact the expert projections range from non-scenario to blackout *proves* <u>anything</u> is possible, from minor inconveniences to total meltdown. There are no <u>genuine</u> experts who

---

80 *Time Bomb 2000* by Edward Yourdon and Jennifer Yourdon, Prentice Hall, Upper Saddle River, NJ 07458.

argue that *all* Y2K related problems will be fixed in time, or even that fixing them all is even possible. It isn't a question of if Y2K will have an impact, but rather one of degrees. And the more severe the impact, the longer the crisis will last.

Prepare for the Unexpected

+ + +

Preparations for Y2K will vary significantly from region to region. During the month of January, most of the country will be firmly in the icy grip of winter. Survival planning for winter conditions means more than just finding some way to keep yourself warm. Most of us immediately think of not freezing to death. So it would seem that the first order of business is staying warm.

But consider how the cold weather might affect any advance preparations you have already made. Sure, you stored adequate supplies of food and water. But did you consider how you would keep your water supply from freezing once the heat goes off? What about your plumbing? The pipes that supply water to your house are built into the walls of your home. Without heat, those pipes will burst. *Now* is the time to add insulation, not later. FEMA recommends wrapping them in newspaper. People in climates where the wind chill can drop below 40 degrees Fahrenheit know better. Most hardware stores carry insulation especially designed to protect exposed pipes. Consider the expense of doing it *right* now, against effecting repairs *after* the water pressure returns and the burst pipes begin to leak.

What about your canned goods? How will you protect them from freezing? Have you prepared for the unusual? Your preparations may be adequate for ordinary winter conditions, but what about a blizzard or other winter storm conditions? You've thought about an electric generator, a wood stove, and other basic survival equipment. Something as simple as failing to store your stores of food and water in a warm place would undo months of Y2K preparation, putting you back at square one *after* it's too late to start over!

If you live in an area prone to flooding when sewers back up, evaluate the threat posed to your property in the event the flow is interrupted by pumping failures and prepare an appropriate response.

Some parts of our infrastructure are so routine that they become transparent. It's easy to plan for a blackout, candles, flashlights, batteries, etc., because most of us have experienced local outages as the results of storms or other natural disasters. But we are unprepared, experientially, for anything approaching the kind of sustained and utter meltdown that Y2K has the potential of causing.

Develop a Checklist
+ + +

Start with an open-ended checklist that you can add to as needed. In the following pages, we'll try and give you some suggestions to get you started, but this is by no means a comprehensive survival guide. Customize your list to meet the needs of your circumstances, locality and pocketbook.

Many of the emergency items that you will need to see you through a sustained Y2K crisis are things that you can pick up as part of your weekly shopping, spreading the expense out over a period of months. **Don't** wait until the last minute to begin filling your inventory! As the year 2000 approaches, and public awareness increases, shortages of some critical supplies will be inevitable!

There aren't enough gasoline powered electrical generators to equip every home in America, and, as existing supplies dwindle, there may not be enough money in America to buy one when you need it! Canned goods, emergency rations, flashlight batteries and medical supplies may also run short well in advance of need.

Y2K Survival—The Basics
+ + +

There are all kinds of degrees of preparation for Y2K, from a few simple precautions to building a fortress in a rural area. Obviously, some of us can afford much less than others. But just because you *can't* afford a private fortress, doesn't mean that you can't take *any* preparations to safeguard your family and property.

Make your survival checklist manageable. Separate items into two categories—the basic essentials and the more expensive survival equipment.

Fill the basics list first. A kerosene cookstove is a wise investment—but not if you forget to buy fuel. Canned goods are a life-saver, but not if your only can opener is electric. Create an "A" list, and fill it before you move on to your "B" list with more expensive items that are less critical. If you've spent all your money on alternative sources of heat and energy before you get all the basics like food and water in place, all you have accomplished is supply a comfortable environment to starve to death in. You might want to consider buying a food dehydrator now, and start preparing your own store of dried foods in advance. Dried foods will keep much longer, and require less storage space. And preparing your own dehydrated rations will save you money that you can then put toward some of the more expensive survival equipment.

A portable electric generator is a good investment, but is it a lifesaver? (It might be if you forgot to buy a manual can opener) But if all you want a generator for is to keep the lights on at night, candles are cheaper. You may have to make some compromises. Budget the luxuries *last*. Here are a few survival dos and don'ts in the event of a catastrophic Y2K failure.

- Stockpile some food. Even if nothing else happens, expect a last minute panic rush on the stores. Be prepared to go at least several weeks with empty store shelves and no restocking in sight.
- Stockpile some drinking water. If the power grid goes down, the water will stop flowing out of the taps.
- Think about how you will stay warm without power in January. If you live in a cold climate, there is a very real danger of freezing to death in your own home.
- Have enough cash on hand to last for several weeks. Don't expect credit cards or checks to be accepted anywhere. Don't expect ATMs to be working. Do expect price gouging and profiteering.
- Don't fly. Military and commercial planes may or may not fall out of the sky when their on-board computers tick over at midnight, but the air traffic control system is sure to crash. The FAA is very far behind on Y2K compliance. They don't expect to

be done until years into the next century.

•Stay away from nuclear power plants. The NRC may force them to shut down in the days or hours before Y2K, but whatever happens, don't stay downwind from one.

•Stay out of elevators between 31/12/99 and whenever things settle down. Remember elevators are controlled by computers. Even if the computers don't fail, you will be stuck if the power goes out. Keep in mind that the elevator you are stuck in is just one of hundreds—or thousands of elevators that also stopped working. It may be some time before all of them have been checked for people trapped inside. You're much better off taking the stairs than spending as much as several days in a darkened elevator car.

•Stay out of subways. Unless you enjoy being trapped in the dark deep underground with hundreds of strangers.

•Stockpile candles, lanterns, flashlights and batteries. Remember, without power, it gets dark after sundown.

•Top off your car's gas tank. Gas pumps don't work without power, and fuel deliveries may be delayed.

•Befriend your neighbors. Pool your resources. Help each other.

Your Y2K Checklist

+ + +

Your checklist should be something you re-evaluate periodically as more information becomes available regarding those parts of the infrastructure that are most likely to experience serious Millennium Bug problems. As we cross the critical "pre-Millennium Bug" dates like April 1 or September 9, 1999, we will have a clearer idea of those areas where the Bug will hit the hardest. Be conscious of how those failures may cascade into problems for you, and ensure your readiness checklist reflects the threat.

For example, if your utility company begins experiencing problems early, you may be well served to push up your planned purchase of a portable electrical generator while the supply is still relatively stable. If your bank begins to experience bookkeeping problems related to the approaching century date change, maybe you might want to consider converting your bank accounts to a more liquid form (like cash or silver or gold coins) in advance of a bank panic that could dry up the available supply before you get a chance to get yours. Stay vigilant, and keep your powder dry.

I Don't Feel So Good!

+ + +

On this side of Y2K, those words trigger a predictable series of events in most families. When my kids got sick, I'd first feel their forehead, then take their temperature. Next would be the call to the doctor, who would prescribe whatever was necessary to take care of the problem. A trip to the drug store usually meant problem solved! In an extreme case, a trip to the emergency room would come first, and then, off to the drug store.

Notice there are several things that may not be possible on January 1, 2000. You can't call the doctor if the phones don't work. You can't drive to the drug store if your car is one of those susceptible to Y2K. You can't pick up your prescription if the drug store is unable to order supplies or fill your order. You can't go to the emergency room if it has been closed by the Bug.

•**Make Sure You Stockpile Critical Prescriptions** Millions of diabetics require the drug insulin. Seventy percent of the world's supply of this substance is produced in a single manufacturing plant in the Netherlands. This plant must be a marvel of efficiency to have captured such a large share of the world market. In today's competitive world this degree of efficiency is seldom possible without the extensive use computers—lots of computers. The world's diabetics are betting their lives on the Y2K status of those computers.

•Have a Well Stocked First Aid Kit Handy

Accidents happen in the best of times, and it's a good idea to have a first aid kit handy even if an ambulance is just a phone call away. But what if the ambulances aren't running and the hospitals can't function? What if there's no way to get to a doctor immediately?

There are many excellent first aid handbooks that will not only help you to select those indispensables that you need for your first aid kit, but also will supply you with some step-by-step first aid techniques. It's a good idea to take an emergency first aid course, as well. You never know if you're going to need it, but if you DO need it, it will be too late to wish you had.

Make sure your emergency first aid kit contains at least the following items. (This is not a comprehensive list—consider what other items you may need for your own family's individual medical problems.)

- •Sterile adhesive bandages in assorted sizes
- •2-inch sterile gauze pads (4-6)
- •4-inch sterile gauze pads (4-6)
- •Hypo allergenic adhesive tape
- •Triangular bandages (3)
- •2-inch sterile roller bandages (3 rolls)

- 3-inch sterile roller bandages (3 rolls)
- Scissors
- Tweezers
- Needle
- Moistened towelettes
- Antiseptic
- Thermometer
- Tongue blades (2)
- Tube of petroleum jelly or other lubricant
- Assorted sizes of safety pins
- Cleansing agent/soap
- Latex gloves (2 pair)
- Sunscreen
- Non-prescription drugs
- Aspirin or non-aspirin pain reliever
- Anti-diarrhea medication
- Antacid (for stomach upset)
- Syrup of Ipecac (use to induce vomiting if advised by the Poison Control Center)
- Laxative
- Activated charcoal (use if advised by the Poison Control Center)

Financial Preparations

+ + +

If you follow a few simple rules for preparing yourself to meet the financial crisis that will certainly follow any sustained Y2K shutdowns, you may weather the storm. But remember that the financial crunch will be just as severe for your creditors, and they will need to collect as much as they can in order to survive themselves. In addition, every open revolving charge is susceptible to Y2K date miscalculations that could interpret your very modest VISA bill as being 100 years overdue. By the time you establish that you only owe $79.12 instead of $3,988,341.16 their computer *says* you owe, you may already be on the street.

Rule #1 Get out of debt—now. If you are saddled with credit card and other debt, all your preparations for surviving the crisis may come to nothing. Make sure that whatever you have is protected from creditors.

Rule #2 Make sure you have hard copies of your most recent bill statements. It will be much easier to convince a creditor that your bill is $79.12 instead of $3,988,341.16 if you have your last correct monthly statement to prove it.

Rule #3 Ensure that you have hard copies of any financial instruments, stocks, bonds, etc., for the same reason as Rule #2.

Rule #4 Reexamine your investments. Paper investments of any kind will be risky after January 1, 2000. As more and more investors become aware of the potential risks to the heavily computerized stock market, they will begin to move their money to safer havens—even before January 1. That could trigger an early collapse of the market. If you do want to keep your money in investments, consider government T-bills over the more risky instruments like mutual funds or money market funds.

Rounding Out Your List
+ + +

The most difficult aspect of preparing a survival kit for conditions unknown is remembering the transparencies. Transparencies are items that you use every day but never think about until you need them. Here are a few examples of things other than food, water, and medicine that you may overlook if you aren't careful.

Supplies

- •Mess kits, or paper cups, plates and plastic utensils (you don't want to waste drinking water washing dishes!)
- •Disposable baby bottle liners
- •Flashlight and extra batteries
- •Non-electric can opener, utility knife
- •Matches (a waterproof container is useful as well)
- •Aluminum foil (better than dirtying pans)
- •Plastic storage containers
- •Needles, thread

- Medicine dropper
- Shut-off wrench, to turn off household gas and water
- Candles, lamps and lamp oil
- Battery operated smoke alarm
- Plastic sheeting (in case of leaks, etc.)

Sanitation

- Toilet paper, towelettes (especially for babies)
- Soap, liquid detergent (antibacterial soap that doesn't use water is available)
- Feminine supplies
- Personal hygiene items (especially deodorant!)
- Baby needs (diapers, ointments, etc.)
- Contact lenses and solution
- Denture needs
- Extra eyeglasses
- Plastic garbage bags, ties, various sizes (for personal sanitation uses, etc.)
- Plastic buckets with tight lids (serve as great potties!)
- Disinfectant
- Household chlorine bleach
- Room deodorizer (spray or solid. No wall plug-ins!)

What About Rover?
+ + +

When making preparations, what about the family pet? Depending on circumstances, you may find yourself having to choose whether or not there is enough food for both your family and Rover.

Consider adding the following to your Survival List. Food (canned and dried), chew toys (you don't want Rover chewing up the insulation because he's bored), pet vitamins, kitty litter or newspapers, and bedding. You will already have plenty of stress without the added tension of having to choose between your survival and the needs of good, old, loyal Rover! Start now, while you can still afford it. Remember, Rover is more than just a pet. A barking dog can be all that is necessary to convince would-be food marauders that maybe the pickings might be easier elsewhere.

Epilogue
+ + +

We've looked at what the Y2K bug is, its potential threat, and discussed some things you can do to prepare yourself and your family. Now, it's time to talk about the most important preparation of all, your spiritual preparation.

Folks, one of the saddest things is that the Christian world is most resistant to prepare for this problem. I feel the information we've given in this book is essential information everyone needs to have in order to make adequate preparations. But, though we may prepare in every way—and I think they should—there's still another preparation that's most important of all.

The Bible says,[81] "Be careful for nothing, [*do not be worried, literally*] but in everything by prayer and supplication with thanksgiving let your requests be made known unto God. And the peace of God, which passeth all understanding, shall keep your hearts and minds through Christ Jesus."

You know the most important thing that we can learn right now is that the promises of God are more real than those problems that are before us. He will carry our anxieties, worries, and fears, and that's especially applicable to what we are heading into. In the Epistle to the Hebrews we're told: "Let us therefore fear, lest, a promise being left us of entering into His rest, any of you should seem to come short of it" (Hebrews 4:1).

Now this means that God has left many, many promises for us to be used here in time, and that we are to claim those promises in time of need. The Bible contains many illustrations of this principle of trusting in God in times of trouble. One

---

81 Philippians 4:6-7 KJV.

historical illustration is that of the time of Moses when God led the children of Israel out of Egypt. They knew God was leading them; they could see His Manifest Presence as it shone before them like a beacon in the night. Despite the fact that they *knew* that God Himself was in the lead, still, God deliberately presented them with one test after another. This historical incident, and others as they moved through the Sinai, received the Law of Moses, and went on to the final destination of the Promised Land—all of these things were deliberately presented. He was preparing them for their journey and eventual arrival in the Promised Land, where they would truly have to trust the promises of God for their survival.

Now, one of those tests was very severe. God led them to a place of seeming safety, well along the way. But the place where He led them was a cul-de-sac. Their backs were to the Red Sea, and on the north and the south. But they were happy and knew that God was taking care of them. Suddenly, they looked up to see a column of cavalry, along with a column of the finest mechanized troops of the ancient world, bearing down on them, blocking the only avenue of escape!

So, what did the fleeing Hebrews do? They *knew* that God led them there. They had reached their destination by following His Presence. They *knew* that God had promised to protect them and to see them safely all the way to the Promised Land.

But what they *saw* was the rapidly approaching Egyptian army. They were trapped! What did God expect them to do? What God expected them to do was to trust in His promises. It was a test. Did they look to God for their salvation? No, they turned on Moses for leading them to this trap. They told him that they wished he had left them as slaves in Egypt, where they were at least fed and cared for by the Egyptians. It didn't take them very long to fail the faith test!

But sometimes, it only takes one faithful man to man to accomplish God's purpose and affect the lives of millions of people. In this case, that man was Moses, who looked out over the Red Sea.

God commanded Moses to raise his staff, and the Red Sea opened before them, opening a path of escape from the approaching Egyptian troops. God made a promise, and He kept it, despite the faithlessness of the Israelites. God is faithful to keep His promises, whether or not we keep ours! The Israelites were facing certain death at the hands of the Egyptians. They were trapped with no way out. At the last minute, God Himself provided the way out.

Y2K is a little like the approaching Egyptian army. And we are often like the Israelites, who looked to God in times of safety, and who despair as soon as something comes up that looks too big for God to handle.

It isn't very hard to have faith when times are good—sometimes, we even forget and take credit for the good times themselves. God usually gets credit for earthquakes, or hurricanes, or floods—the kinds of things insurance policies term "acts of God." But while we give Him the credit for hard times, we forget His promise to see us through them. When God tested the Israelites, He wasn't testing their spelling or arithmetic. He tested whether or not they were ready to proceed to the next waypoint on their journey. It wasn't that God didn't already know. The test was because *they* didn't know, so God created a situation to prove His faithfulness in spite of their lack of faith.

The Bible says that "faith is the expectation of things hoped for, and the substance of things not seen." For example, a factory worker has *faith* that his paycheck will come on Friday afternoon. He *expects* it to contain the compensation promised him. But he hasn't *seen* it, and he won't—until Friday, when he has earned it.

Trusting—or having faith—in the promises of God is no more complicated than waiting for payday. I have faith in what I *hope for*—that God has already made provision for me according to His plan, so I needn't be afraid of whatever happens, even Y2K. The fact that God has *already* promised means that I can count on it, as surely as the worker counts on payday, even though God hasn't already shown me just how he will handle the situation.

Many pre-Tribulation Christians mistakenly believe that somehow nothing bad will happen until after the Rapture, since the Tribulation doesn't begin until sometime after that. Unfortunately, that's not doctrine; that's dreaming. There is nothing to say that the Church will be spared from the trials that are part of day-to-day living, but only that the Church will be raptured *before* the man of sin is revealed.

The Bible promises that "in this world you shall have tribulation, but be of good cheer, I [Jesus] have overcome the world."

The Bible contains more than 7000 promises from God—promises that God is faithful to keep. All you have to do is claim them. Unfortunately, too many Christians are like the Israelites of the Exodus. We *know* God is in control, we *know* He led us to where we are, and we *know* He has a plan. But what we *see* is Y2K, bearing down on us like Pharaoh's troops. The Israelites were hemmed in on three sides with their backs to the sea. Like the Israelites, we too are trapped. With shortsightedness on one side, complacency on the other, and our backs to the clock and the looming Millennial Bug cutting off any avenue of escape. The Israelites blamed Moses. We blame programmers. Moses looked to the promises of God. We look to programmers for a "magic bullet."

There is no magic bullet. But God remains—and He remains faithful to His promises. God promised us that whoever wants to come under His umbrella of protection need only ask. Take a minute, right now, and consider the situation. Do you *really* want to go it alone? Or would you prefer to follow the same guiding Beacon that led the Israelites through test after test, only to see them safely to the Promised Land?

Along the shore of the Red Sea that day two enemies faced each other. Egypt trusted in weapons and equipment and plenty of manpower. The Israelites rested safely in the promises of God.

God made a promise to you, as well. He promised that He would send His only Son to stand in your place, as Moses stood in place of the Israelites faithlessness, and to lead you, under His protection, through the coming tests along the road to the Promised Land. Right where you are, if you want to know that "peace that surpasses all understanding," call out to

Jesus. Ask Him to lead you in the direction that He would have you to go. Believe His promise that He will never leave you nor forsake you. Know the thrill of trading the cares of this world for the certainty of His Promises. If you accept the free gift of pardon and fellowship that Jesus has purchased on your behalf, then your Y2K preparedness program is complete.

Tally Ho!

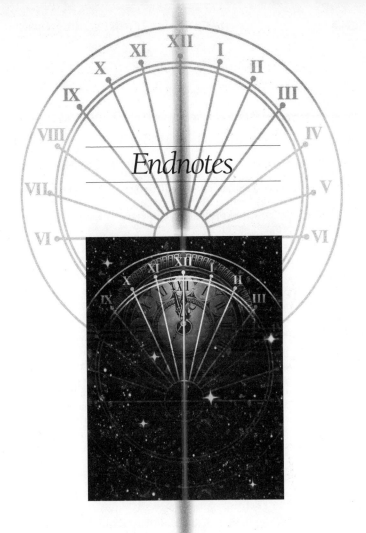

Endnotes

EXECUTIVE ORDER   EO 12919
Effective Date: June 3, 1994

Responsible Office: ID

Subject: NATIONAL DEFENSE INDUSTRIAL RESOURCES
        PREPAREDNESS

TEXT

By the authority vested in me as President by the Constitution and
the laws of the United States of America, including the Defense
Production Act of 1950, as amended (64 Stat. 798; 50 U.S.C. App.
2061, et. seq.) and section 301 of title 3, United States Code, and
as Commander in Chief of the Armed Forces of the United States,
it is hereby ordered as follows:

PART 1 — PURPOSE, POLICY AND IMPLEMENTATION

Section 101. Purpose. This order delegates authorities and
addresses national defense industrial resource policies and programs under the Defense Production Act of 1950, as amended
("the Act"), except for the amendments to Title III of the Act in the
Energy Security Act of 1980 and telecommunication authorities
under Executive Order No. 12472.

Sec. 102. Policy. The United States must have an industrial and
technology base capable of meeting national defense requirements,
and capable of contributing to the technological superiority of its
defense equipment in peacetime and in times of national emergency. The domestic industrial and technological base is the foundation for national defense preparedness. The authorities provided
in the Act shall be used to strengthen this base and to ensure it is
capable of responding to all threats to the national security of the
United States.

Sec. 103. General Functions. Federal departments and agencies
responsible for defense acquisition (or for industrial resources
needed to support defense acquisition) shall:

(a) Identify requirements for the full spectrum of national
security emergencies, including military, industrial, and
essential civilian demand;

(b) Assess continually the capability of the domestic
industrial and technological base to satisfy requirements
in peacetime and times of national emergency, specifically
evaluating the availability of adequate industrial resource
and production sources, including subcontractors and
suppliers materials, skilled labor, and professional and
technical personnel;

(c) Be prepared, in the event of a potential threat to the
security of the United States, to take actions necessary to
ensure the availability of adequate industrial resources
and production capability, including services and critical
technology for national defense requirements;

(d) Improve the efficiency and responsiveness to defense requirements of the domestic industrial base; and

(e) Foster cooperation between the defense and commercial sectors for research and development and for acquisition of materials, components and equipment to enhance industrial base efficiency and responsiveness

Sec. 104. Implementation. (a) The National Security Council is the principal forum for consideration and resolution of national security resource preparedness policy.

(b) The Director, Federal Emergency Management Agency ("Director FEMA") shall:

(1) Serve as an advisor to the National Security Council on issues of national security resource preparedness and on the use of the authorities and functions delegated by this order.

(2) Provide for the central coordination of the plans and programs incident to authorities and functions delegated under this order, and provide guidance and procedures approved by the Assistant to the President for National Security Affairs to the Federal departments and agencies under this order.

(3) Establish procedures, in consultation with Federal departments and agencies assigned functions under this order, to resolve in a timely and effective manner conflicts and issues that may arise in implementing the authorities and functions delegated under this order; and

(4) Report to the President periodically concerning all program activities conducted pursuant to this order.

(c) The head of every Federal department and agency assigned functions under this order shall ensure that the performance of these functions is consistent with National Security Council policy and guidelines.

PART II — PRIORITIES AND ALLOCATIONS

Sec. 201. Delegations of Priorities and Allocations. (a) The authority of the President conferred by section 101 of the Act to require acceptance and priority performance of contracts or orders (other than contracts of employment) to promote the national defense over performance of any other contracts or orders, and to allocate materials, services, and facilities as deemed necessary or appropriate to promote the national defense, is delegated to the following agency heads:

(1) The Secretary of Agriculture with respect to food resources, food resource facilities, and the

domestic distribution of farm equipment and commercial fertilizer;

(2) The Secretary of Energy with respect to all forms of energy;

(3) The Secretary of Health and Human Services with respect to health resources;

(4) The Secretary of Transportation with respect to all forms of civil transportation;

(5) The Secretary of Defense with respect to water resources; and

(6) The Secretary of Commerce for all other materials, services, and facilities, including construction materials.

(b) The Secretary of Commerce, in consultation with the heads of those departments and agencies specified in subsection 201(a) of this order, shall administer the Defense Priorities and Allocations System ("DPAS") regulations that will be used to implement the authority of the President conferred by section 101 of the Act as delegated to the Secretary of Commerce in subsection 201(a)(6) of this order. The Secretary of Commerce will redelegate to the Secretary of Defense, and the heads of other departments and agencies as appropriate, authority for the priority rating of contracts and others for all materials, services, and facilities needed in support of programs approved under section 202 of this order. The Secretary of Commerce shall act as appropriate upon Special Priorities Assistance requests in a time frame consistent with the urgency of the need at hand.

(c) The Director, FEMA, shall attempt to resolve issues or disagreements on priorities or allocations between Federal departments or agencies in a time frame consistent with the urgency of the issue at hand, and if not resolved, such issues will be referred to the Assistant to the President for National Security Affairs for final determination.

(d) The head of each Federal department or agency assigned functions under subsection 201(a) of this order, when necessary, shall make the finding required under subsection 101(b) of the Act. This finding shall be submitted for the President's approval through the Assistant to the President for National Security Affairs. Upon such approval the head of the Federal department or agency that made the finding may use the authority of subsection 101(a) of the Act to control the general distribution of any material (including applicable services) in the civilian market.

(e) The Assistant to the President for National Security Affairs is hereby delegated the authority under subsection

101(c)(3) of the Act, and will be assisted by the Director, FEMA, in ensuring the coordinated administration of the Act.

Sec. 202. Determinations. The authority delegated by section 201 of this order may be used only to support programs that have been determined in writing as necessary or appropriate to promote the national defense:

(a) By the Secretary of Defense with respect to military production and construction, military assistance to foreign nations, stockpiling, outer space, and directly related activities;

(b) By the Secretary of Energy with respect to energy production and construction, distribution and use, and directly related activities; and

(c) By the Director, FEMA, with respect to essential civilian needs supporting national defense, including civil defense and continuity of government and directly related activities.

Sec. 203. Maximizing Domestic Energy Supplies. The authority of the President to perform the functions provided by subsection 101(c) of the Act is delegated to the Secretary of Commerce, who shall redelegate to the Secretary of Energy the authority to make the findings described in subsection 101(c)(2)(A) that the materials (including equipment), services, and facilities are critical and essential. The Secretary of Commerce shall make the finding described in subsection 101(c)(2)(A) of the Act that the materials (including equipment), services, or facilities are scarce, and the finding described in subsection 101(c)(2)(B) that it is necessary to use the authority provided by subsection 101(c)(1).

Sec. 204. Chemical and Biological Warfare. The authority of the President conferred by subsection 104(b) of the Act is delegated to the Secretary of Defense. This authority may not be further delegated by the Secretary.

PART III — EXPANSION OF PRODUCTIVE CAPACITY AND SUPPLY

Sec. 301. (a) Financing Institution Guarantees. To expedite or expand production and deliveries or services under government contracts for the procurement of industrial resources or critical technology items essential to the national defense, the head of each Federal department or agency engaged in procurement for the national defense (referred to as "agency head" in this part) and the President and Chairman of the Export-Import Bank of the United States (in cases involving capacity expansion, technological development, or production in foreign countries) are authorized to guarantee in whole or in part any public or private financing institution, subject to provisions of section 301 of the Act. Guarantees shall be made in consultation with the Department of the Treasury as to the terms and conditions thereof. The Director of the Office of Management and Budget ("OMB") shall be informed when such guarantees are to be made.

(b) Direct Loan Guarantees. To expedite or expand production and deliveries or services under government contracts for the procurement of industrial resources or critical technology items essential to the national defense, each agency head is authorized to make direct loan guarantees from funds appropriated to their agency for Title III.

(c) Fiscal Agent. Each Federal Reserve Bank is designated and authorized to act, on behalf of any guaranteeing agency, as fiscal agent in the making of guarantee contracts and in otherwise carrying out the purposes of section 301 of the Act.

(d) Regulations. The Board of Governors of the Federal Reserve System is authorized, after consultation with heads of guaranteeing departments and agencies, the Secretary of the Treasury, and the Director, OMB, to prescribe regulations governing procedures, forms, rates of interest, and fees for such guarantee contracts.

Sec. 302. Loans. (a) To expedite production and deliveries or services to aid in carrying out government contracts for the procurement of industrial resources or a critical technology item for the national defense, an agency head is authorized, subject to the provisions of section 302 of the Act, to submit to the Secretary of the Treasury or the President and Chairman of the Export-Import Bank of the United States (in cases involving capacity expansion, technological development, or production in foreign countries) applications for loans.

(b) To expedite or expand production and deliveries or services under government contracts for the procurement of industrial resources or critical technology items essential to the national defense, each agency head may make direct loans from funds appropriated to their agency for Title III.

(c) After receiving a loan application and determining that financial assistance is not otherwise available on reasonable terms, the Secretary of the Treasury or the President and Chairman of the Export-Import Bank of the United States (in cases involving capacity expansion, technological development, or production in foreign countries) may make loans, subject to provisions of section 302 of the Act.

Sec. 303. Purchase Commitments. (a) In order to carry out the objectives of the Act, and subject to the provisions of section 303 thereof, an agency head is authorized to make provision for purchases of, or commitments to purchase, an industrial resource or a critical technology item for government use or resale.

(b) Materials acquired under section 303 of the Act that exceed the needs of the programs under the Act may be transferred to the National Defense Stockpile, if such transfer is determined by the Secretary of Defense as the National Defense Stockpile Manager to be in the public interest.

Sec. 304. Subsidy Payments. In order to ensure the supply of raw or non-processed materials from high-cost sources, an agency head is authorized to make subsidy payments, after consultation with the Secretary of the Treasury and the Director, OMB, and subject to the provisions of section 303(c) of the Act.

Sec. 305. Determinations and Findings. When carrying out the authorities in sections 301 through 303 of this order, an agency head is authorized to make the required determinations, judgments, statements, certifications, and findings, in consultation with the Secretary of Defense, Secretary of Energy or Director, FEMA, as appropriate. The agency head shall provide a copy of the determination, judgment, statement, certification, or finding to the Director, OMB, to the Director, FEMA, and, when appropriate, to the Secretary of the Treasury.

Sec. 306. Strategic and Critical Materials. (a) The Secretary of the Interior in consultation with the Secretary of Defense as the National Defense Stockpile Manager and subject to the provisions of section 303 of the Act, is authorized to encourage the exploration, development, and mining of critical and strategic materials and other materials.

(b) An agency head is authorized, pursuant to section 303(g) of the Act, to make provision for the development of substitutes for strategic and critical materials, critical components, critical technology items, and other industrial resources to aid the national defense.

(c) An agency head is authorized, pursuant to section 303(a)(1)(B) of the Act, to make provisions to encourage the exploration, development and mining of critical and strategic materials and other materials.

Sec. 307. Government-owned Equipment. An agency head is authorized, pursuant to section 303(e) of the Act, to install additional equipment facilities, processes, or improvements to facilities owned by the government and to install government-owned equipment in industrial facilities owned by private persons.

Sec. 308. Identification of Shortfalls. Except during periods of national emergency or after a Presidential determination in accordance with sections 301(e)(1)(D)(ii), 302(c)(4)(B), or 303(a)(7)(B) of the Act, no guarantee, loan or other action pursuant to sections 301, 302, 303 of the Act to correct an industrial shortfall shall be taken unless the shortfall has been identified in the Budget of the United States or amendments thereto.

Sec.309. Defense Production Act Fund Manager. The Secretary of Defense is designated the Defense Production Act Fund Manager, in accordance with section 304(f) of the Act, and shall carry out the duties specified in that section, in consultation with the agency heads having approved Title III projects and appropriated Title III funds.

Sec. 310. Critical Items List. (a) Pursuant to section 107(b)(1)(A) of the Act, the Secretary of Defense shall identify critical components and critical technology items for each item on the Critical Items List of the Commanders-in-Chief of the Unified and Specified Commands and other items within the inventory of weapon systems and defense equipment.

> (b) Each agency head shall take appropriate action to ensure that critical components or critical technology items are available from reliable sources when needed to meet defense requirements during peacetime, graduated mobilization, and national emergency. "Appropriate action" may include restricting contract solicitations to reliable sources, restricting contract solicitations to domestic sources (pursuant to statutory authority), stockpiling critical components, and developing substitutes for critical components or critical technology items.

Sec. 311. Strengthening Domestic Capability. An agency head, in accordance with section 107(a) of the Act, may utilize the authority of Title III of the Act or any other provision of law, in consultation with the Secretary of Defense, to provide appropriate incentives to develop, maintain, modernize, and expand the productive capacities of domestic sources for critical components, critical technology items, and industrial resources essential for the execution of the national security strategy of the United States.

Sec. 312. Modernization of Equipment. An agency head, in accordance with section 108(b) of the Act, may utilize the authority of Title III of the Act to guarantee the purchase or lease of advance manufacturing equipment and any related services with respect to any such equipment for purposes of the Act.

PART IV—IMPACT OF OFFSETS

Sec. 401. Offsets. (a) The responsibilities and authority conferred upon the President by section 309 of the Act with respect to offsets are delegated to the Secretary of Commerce, who shall function as the President's Executive Agency for carrying out this authority.

> (b) The Secretary of Commerce shall prepare the annual report required by section 309(a) of the Act in consultation with the Secretaries of Defense, Treasury, Labor, State, the United States Trade Representative, the Arms Control and Disarmament Agency, the Director of Central Intelligence, and the heads of other departments and

agencies as required. The heads of Federal departments and agencies shall provide the Secretary of Commerce with such information as may be necessary for the effective performance of this function.

(c) The offset report shall be subject to the normal interagency clearance process conducted by the Director, OMB prior to the report's submission by the President to Congress.

PART V—VOLUNTARY AGREEMENTS
AND ADVISORY COMMITTEES

Sec. 501. Appointments. The authority of the President under sections 708(c) and (d) of the Act is delegated to the heads of each Federal department or agency, except that, insofar as that authority relates to section 101 of the Act, it is delegated only to the heads of each Federal department or agency assigned functions under section 201(a) of this order. The authority delegated under this section shall be exercised pursuant to the provisions of section 708 of the Act, and copies and the status of the use of such delegations shall be furnished to the Director, FEMA.

Sec. 502. Advisory Committees. The authority of the President under section 708(d) of the Act and delegated in section 501 of this order (relating to establishment of advisory committees) shall be exercised only after consultation with, and in accordance with, guidelines and procedures established by the Administrator of General Services.

PART VI—EMPLOYMENT OF PERSONNEL

Sec. 601. National Defense Executive Reserve. (a) In accordance with section 710(e) of the Act, there is established in the Executive Branch a National Defense Executive Reserve ("NDER") composed of persons of recognized expertise from various segments of the private sector and from government (except full-time federal employees) for training for employment in executive positions in the Federal Government in the event of an emergency that requires such employment.

(b) The head of any department or agency may establish a unit of the NDER in the department or agency and train members of that unit.

(c) The head of each department or agency with an NDER unit is authorized to exercise the President's authority to employ civilian personnel in accordance with section 703(a) of the Act when activating all or a part of its NDER unit. The exercise of this authority shall be subject to the provisions of subsections 601(d) and (e) of this order and shall not be redelegated.

(d) The head of a department or agency may activate an NDER unit, in whole or in part, upon the written determination that an emergency affecting the national security or defense preparedness of the United States exists and that the activation of the unit is necessary to carry out the emergency program functions of the department or agency.

(e) At least 72 hours prior to activating the NDER unit, the head of the department or agency shall notify, in writing, the Assistant to the President for National Security Affairs of the impending activation and provide a copy of the determination required under subsection 601(d) of this order.

(f) The Director, FEMA, shall coordinate the NDER program activities of departments and agencies in establishing units of the Reserve; provide for appropriate guidance for recruitment, training, and activation; and issue necessary rules and guidance in connection with the program.

(g) This order suspends any delegated authority, regulation, or other requirement or condition with respect to the activation of any NDER unit, in whole or in part, or appointment of any NDER member that is inconsistent with the authorities delegated herein, provided that the aforesaid suspension applies only as long as sections 703(a) and 710(e) of the Act are in effect.

Sec. 602. Consultants. The head of each department or agency assigned functions under this order is delegated authority under sections 710(b) and (c) of the Act to employ persons of outstanding experience and ability without compensation and to employ experts, consultants, or organizations, the authority delegated by this section shall not be redelegated.

PART VII—LABOR SUPPLY

Sec. 701. Secretary of Labor. The Secretary of Labor, identified in this section as the Secretary, shall:

(a) Collect, analyze, and maintain data needed to make a continuing appraisal of the nation's labor requirements and the supply of workers for purposes of national defense. All agencies of the government shall cooperate with the Secretary in furnishing information necessary for this purpose, to the extent permitted by law;

(b) In response to requests from the head of a Federal department or agency engaged in the procurement for national defense, consult with and advise the department or agency with respect to (1) the effect of contemplated actions on labor supply and utilization, (2) the relation of labor supply to materials and facilities requirements, and (3) such other matters as will assist in making the exercise of priority and allocations functions consistent with effective utilization and distribution of labor;

(c) Formulate plans, programs, and policies for meeting defense and essential civilian labor requirements;

(d) Project skill shortages to facilitate meeting defense and essential civilian needs and establish training programs;

(e) Determine the occupations and skills critical to meeting the labor requirements of defense and essential civilian activities and, with the assistance of the Secretary of Defense, the Director of Selective Service, and such other persons as the Director, FEMA, may designate, develop policies regulating the induction and deferment of personnel for the armed services, except for civilian personnel in the reserves; and

(f) Administer an effective labor-management relations policy to support the activities and programs under this order with the cooperation of other Federal agencies, including the National Labor Relations Board and the Federal Mediation and Conciliation Service.

PART VIII — DEFENSE INDUSTRIAL BASE INFORMATION AND REPORTS

Sec. 801. Foreign Acquisition of Companies. The Secretary of the Treasury, in cooperation with the Department of State, the Department of Defense, the Department of Commerce, the Department of Energy, the Department of Agriculture, the Attorney General, and the Director of Central Intelligence, shall complete and furnish a report to the President and then to Congress in accordance with the requirements of section 721(k) of the Act concerning foreign efforts to acquire United States companies involved in research, development, or production of critical technologies and industrial espionage activities directed by foreign governments against private U.S. companies.

Sec. 802. Defense Industrial Base Information System. (a) The Secretary of Defense and the heads of other appropriate Federal departments and agencies, as determined by the Secretary of Defense, shall establish an information system on the domestic defense industrial base in accordance with the requirements of section 722 of the Act.

(b) In establishing the information system required by subsection (a) of this order, the Secretary of Defense, the Secretary of Commerce, and the heads of other appropriate Federal departments and agencies, as determined by the Secretary of Defense in consultation with the Secretary of Commerce, shall consult with each other for the purposes of performing the duties listed in section 722(d)(1) of the Act.

(c) The Secretary of Defense shall convene a task force consisting of the Secretary of Commerce and the Secretary of each military department and the heads of other appropriate Federal departments and agencies, as determined by the Secretary of Defense in consultation with the Secretary of Commerce, to carry out the duties under section 722(d)(2) of the Act.

(d) The Secretary of Defense shall report to Congress on a strategic plan for developing a cost-effective, comprehensive information system capable of identifying on a timely, ongoing basis vulnerability in critical components and critical technology items. The plans shall include an assessment of the performance and cost-effectiveness of procedures specified in section 722(b) of the Act.

(e) The Secretary of Commerce, acting through the Bureau of the Census, shall consult with the Secretary of Defense and the Director, FEMA, to improve the usefulness of information derived from the Census of Manufacturers in carrying out section 722 of the Act.

(f) The Secretary of Defense shall perform an analysis of the production base for not more than two major weapons systems of each military department in establishing the information system under section 722 of the Act. Each analysis shall identify the critical components of each system.

(g) The Secretary of Defense, in consultation with the Secretary of Commerce, and the heads of other Federal departments and agencies as appropriate, shall issue a biennial report on critical components and technology in accordance with section 722(e) of the Act.

PART IX—GENERAL PROVISIONS

Sec. 901. Definitions. In addition to the definitions in section 702 of the Act, the following definitions apply throughout this order:

(a) "Civil transportation" includes movement of persons and property by all modes of transportation in interstate, intrastate, or foreign commerce within the United States, its territories and possessions, and the District of Columbia, and, without limitation, related public storage and warehousing, ports, services, equipment and facilities, such as transportation carrier shop and repair facilities. However, "civil transportation" shall not include transportation owned or controlled by the Department of Defense, use of petroleum and gas pipelines, and coal slurry pipelines used only to supply energy production facilities directly. As applied herein, "civil transportation" shall include direction, control, and coordination of civil transportation capacity regardless of ownership.

(b) "Energy" means all forms of energy including petroleum, gas (both natural and manufactured), electricity, solid fuels (including all forms of coal, coke, coal chemicals, coal liquification, and coal gasification), and atomic energy, and the production, conservation, use, control and distribution (including pipelines) of all of these forms of energy.

(c) "Farm equipment" means equipment, machinery, and repair parts manufactured for use on farms in connection with the production or preparation for market use of food resources.

(d) "Fertilizer" means any product or combination of products that contain one or more of the elements— nitrogen, phosphorus, and potassium—for use as a plant nutrient.

(e) "Food resources" means all commodities and products, simple, mixed, or compound, or complements to such commodities or products, that are capable of being ingested by either human beings or animals, irrespective of other uses to which such commodities or product may be put, at all stages of processing from the raw commodity to the products thereof in vendible form for human or animal consumption. "Food resources" also means all starches, sugars, vegetable and animal or marine fats and oils, cotton, tobacco, wool mohair, hemp, flax fiber, and naval stores, but does not mean any such material after it loses its identity as an agricultural commodity or agricultural product.

(f) "Food resource facilities" mean plants, machinery, vehicles (including on-farm), and other facilities required for the production, processing distribution, and storage (including cold storage) of food resources, livestock and poultry feed and seed, and for the domestic distribution of farm equipment and fertilizer (excluding transportation thereof).

(g) "Functions" include powers, duties, authority, responsibilities, and discretion.

(h) "Head of each Federal department or agency engaged in procurement for the National defense" means the heads of the Departments of Defense, Energy, and Commerce, as well as those departments and agencies listed in Executive Order No. 10789.

(i) "Heads of other appropriate Federal departments and agencies" as used in part VIII of this order means the heads of such other Federal agencies and departments that acquire information or need information with respect to making any determination to exercise any authority under the Act.

(j) "Health resources" means materials, facilities, health supplies, and equipment (including pharmaceutical, blood collecting and dispensing supplies, biological, surgical textiles, and emergency surgical instruments and supplies) required to prevent the impairment of, improve, or restore the physical and mental health conditions of the population.

(k) "Metals and minerals" means all raw materials of mineral origin (excluding energy) including their refining, smelting, or processing, but excluding their fabrication.

(l) "Strategic and Critical Materials" means materials (including energy) that (1) would be needed to supply the military, industrial, and essential civilian needs of the United States during a national security emergency, and (2) are not found or produced in the United States in sufficient quantities to meet such need and are vulnerable to the termination or reduction of the availability of the material.

(m) "Water resources" means all usable water, from all sources, within the jurisdiction of the United States, which can be managed, controlled, and allocated to meet emergency requirements.

Sec. 902. General. (a) Except as otherwise provided in subsection 902(c) of this order, <u>the authorities vested in the President by title VII of the Act may be exercised and performed by the head of each department and agency in carrying out the delegated authorities under the Act and this order.</u>

(b) The authorities which may be exercised and performed pursuant to subsection 902(a) of this order shall include (1) the power to redelegate authorities, and to authorize to successive redelegation of authorities, to departments and agencies, officers, and employees of the government, and (2) the power of subpoena with respect to authorities delegated in parts II, III, and IV of this order, provided that the subpoena power shall be utilized only after the scope and purpose of the investigation, inspection, or inquiry to which the subpoena relates have been defined either by the appropriate officer identified in subsection 902(a) of this order or by such other person or persons as the officer shall designate.

(c) Excluded from the authorities delegated by subsection 902(a) of this order are authorities delegated by parts V, VI, and VII of this order and the authority with respect to fixing compensation under section 703(a) of the Act.

Sec. 903. Authority. All previously issued orders, regulations, rulings, certificates, directives, and actions relating to any function affected by this order shall remain in effect except as they are inconsistent with this order or are subsequently amended or revoked under proper authority. Nothing in this order shall affect the validity or force of anything done under previous delegations or other assignment of authority under the Act.

Sec. 904. Effect on other Orders. (a) The following are superseded or revoked:

> (1) Section 3, Executive Order No. 8248 of September 8, 1939, (4 FR 3864).
>
> (2) Executive Order No. 10222 of March 8, 1951 (16 FR 2247).
>
> (3) Executive Order No. 10480 of August 14, 1953 (18 FR 4939)
>
> (4) Executive Order No. 10647 of November 28, 1955 (20 FR 8769).
>
> (5) Executive Order No. 11179 of September 22, 1964 (29 FR 13239).
>
> (6) Executive Order No. 11355 of May 26, 1967 (32 FR 7803).
>
> (7) Sections 7 and 8, Executive Order No. 11912 of April 13, 1976 (41 FR 15825, 15826-27).
>
> (8) Section 3, Executive Order No. 12148 of July 20, 1979 (44 FR 43239, 43241).
>
> (9) Executive Order No. 12521 of June 24, 1985 (50 FR 26335).
>
> (10) Executive Order No. 12649 of August 11, 1988 (53 FR 30639.
>
> (11) Executive Order No. 12773 of September 26, 1991 (56 FR 49387), except that part of the order that amends section 604 of Executive Order 10480.

(b) Executive Order No. 10789 of November 14, 1958, is amended by deleting "and in view of the existing national emergency declared by Proclamation No. 2914 of December 16, 1950," as it appears in the first sentence.

(c) Executive Order No. 11790, as amended, relating to the Federal Energy Administration Act of 1974, is amended by deleting "Executive Order No. 10480" where it appears in section 4 and substituting this order's number.

(d) Subject to subsection 904(c) of this order, to the extent that any provision of any prior Executive order is inconsistent with the provisions of this order, this order shall control and such prior provision is amended accordingly.

Sec. 905. Judicial Review. This order is not intended to create any right or benefit, substantive or procedural, enforceable at law by a party against the United States, its agencies, its officers, or any person.

/s/William J. Clinton

THE WHITE HOUSE,
June 3, 1994.

Y2K Readiness Predictions by Country:

Level 1 (15%): Australia, Belgium, Bermuda, Canada, Denmark, Holland, Ireland, Israel, Switzerland, Sweden, UK, US.

Level 2 (33%): Brazil, Chile, Finland, France, Hungary, Italy, Mexico, New Zealand, Norway, Peru, Portugal, Singapore, South Korea, Spain, Taiwan.

Level 3 (50%): Argentina, Armenia, Austria, Bulgaria, Colombia, Czech Republic, Egypt, Germany, Guatemala, India, Japan, Jordan, Kenya, Kuwait, Malaysia, North Korea, Poland, Puerto Rico, Saudi Arabia, South Africa, Sri Lanka, Turkey, UAE (United Arab Emirates), Venezuela, Yugoslavia.

Level 4: (66%): Afghanistan, Bahrain, Bangladesh, Cambodia, Chad, China, Costa Rica, Ecuador, Egypt, El Salvador, Ethiopia, Fiji, Indonesia, Kenya, Laos, Lithuania, Morocco, Mozambique, Nepal, Nigeria, Pakistan, Philippines, Romania, Russia, Somalia, Sudan, Thailand, Uruguay, Vietnam, Zaire, Zimbabwe.

Y2K Readiness Predictions by Industry:

Level 1: Insurance, Investment services, Banking, Pharmaceuticals, Computer Manufacturing.

Level 2: Heavy Equipment, Aerospace, Medical Equipment, Software, Semiconductors, Telecom, Retail, Discrete Manufacturing, Publishing, Biotechnology, Consulting.

Level 3: Chemical Processing, Transportation, Power, Natural Gas, Water, Oil, Law Practices, Medical Practices, Construction, Transportation, Pulp and Paper, Ocean Shipping, Hospitality, Broadcast News, Television, Law Enforcement.

Level 4: Education, Healthcare, Government Agencies, Farming and Agriculture, Food processing, Construction, City and Town Municipal Services.

(Source: GartnerGroup Inc.)

Receive 12 months of the most concise, up-to-date reports from all the hot spots of the world.

Your Access to World Events!

Order your monthly subscription to *International Intelligence Briefing.*

Our worldwide intelligence network has access to news that most Americans never read or hear about, news that is shaping our world. The *International Intelligence Briefing* is vital to Christians who read and believe the Bible; it tracks and accesses world events as they relate to Bible prophecy. Yet even non-Christians will enjoy this briefing because of its unique approach to news about world events and its low-key approach to Christianity and Bible prophecy.

Mailed First Class on the first of each month.

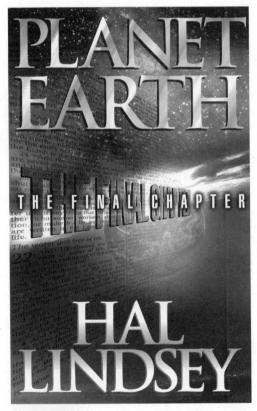